Pantomimes
Charades
& Skits

By VERNON HOWARD

with drawings by SHIZU

 STERLING PUBLISHING CO., INC. NEW YORK

Oak Tree Press Co., Ltd. London & Sydney

BOOKS BY VERNON HOWARD

ACTS FOR COMEDY SHOWS

HOLIDAY MONOLOGUES

HUMOROUS MONOLOGUES

MONOLOGUES FOR BOYS & GIRLS

MONOLOGUES FOR TEENS

MORE CHARADES AND PANTOMIMES

PANTOMIMES , CHARADES AND SKITS

PUPPET AND PANTOMIME PLAYS

SHORT PLAYS FROM THE GREAT CLASSICS

TALKING TO AN AUDIENCE

Revised Edition

Copyright © 1974, 1959 by Sterling Publishing Co., Inc.
419 Park Avenue South, New York, N.Y. 10016
British edition published by Oak Tree Press Co., Ltd., Nassau, Bahamas
Distributed in Australia and New Zealand by Oak Tree Press Co., Ltd.,
P.O. Box J34, Brickfield Hill, Sydney 2000, N.S.W.
Distributed in the United Kingdom and elsewhere in the British Commonwealth
by Ward Lock Ltd., 116 Baker Street, London W 1
Manufactured in the United States of America
All rights reserved
Library of Congress Catalog Card No.: 59–12983
Sterling ISBN 0–8069-7004-9 Trade   Oak Tree 7061–2010-8
7005-7 Library

Contents

Pantomimes

Pantomime is a fascinating and basic form of dramatic art. Once a few rules are understood and applied, amusing pantomimes can easily be staged for the enjoyment of both audience and actors.

No words are spoken during a pantomime performance. All actions take place in total silence. To indicate that you are talking, you may freely move your lips as if speaking, though your lips should not form actual words.

Use as many parts of your body as possible to express an action or a mood or an emotion. For indicating sleepiness you could stretch your arms, rub your eyes, cover a yawn, droop your shoulders, shuffle your feet, lie down, and so forth.

When holding up an imaginary object, be sure to leave space between the fingers, just as if the object were actually in hand. For example, when holding a drinking glass, leave your fingers apart the actual distance of the glass. You can quickly grasp this by first holding a real glass and observing the spacing. The ability to create an illusion of space is aided by actually picking up and setting down the solid objects which you will use, such as a broom, potato, box, then doing the same thing with imaginary objects.

Practice all pantomime movements with actual objects at first. For example, if you are to pantomime the act of removing your coat, take off your own coat several times while observing the movements of your arms and body. Then proceed with the pantomimed version.

A good pantomime actor is always conscious of imaginary scenery and stage properties, such as doors, lamps, tables. This will prevent you from "walking through" a closed door.

Stage properties in pantomime acts are kept at a minimum. Objects such as a ball and a shovel should be imaginary. However, a few objects which are quite necessary to the act—perhaps a chair or table—may be used.

Most pantomime acts can be performed on a bare stage. Backgrounds and scenery, if used at all, should be kept simple. A few flowers or shrubs are enough to indicate an outdoor setting. A sign or two will let the audience know that the scene takes place in a restaurant.

Costumes may be as simple or as fancy as desired. Quite often a single item of dress will reveal the type of character you are playing, such as a feather for an Indian or a badge for a policeman.

SOME EASY GAMES

FOR INTRODUCING PANTOMIME

The following fun-filled games will serve several valuable purposes:

1. They will introduce the players to pantomime.

2. They will enable players to express themselves in a group where no one need feel shy or conspicuous.

3. They will give the players confidence in knowing what they can actually do.

4. They will broaden the players' self-expression through observation of the performance of others.

5. They will give players general experience which can be used in later performances.

USE ALL THAT YOU HAVE!

This amusing stunt will teach players to use all of their faculties for expressing a particular action or mood. Once they see that they need only to use freely those faculties which they *already have*, there will be no stopping them!

Players stand in a circle. The leader or teacher then reads the following movements which express certain actions and attitudes. Players then act them out in pantomime. The leader can greatly assist by first showing them his own exaggerated version.

1. Say with your palm, "Stop!" (raise palm up and outward)

2. Say with your head, "Yes." (nod head)

3. Say with your shoulder, "I bumped the door." (bump shoulder vigorously against imaginary door)

4. Say with your eyes, "I don't understand." (raise eyebrows and blink eyes in bewilderment)

5. Say with your foot, "I'm waiting." (keep heel down, tap toes against floor impatiently)

6. Say with your ear, "I hear a songbird." (tilt ear upward and look up sideways)

7. Say with your waist, "I'm dancing." (sway hips)

8. Say with your jaw, "I'm surprised." (suddenly drop jaw)

9. Say with your tongue (no words), "I like this cake." (roll tongue around lips)

10. Say with your finger, "Come here." (beckon coyly with finger)

11. Say with your arms, "I'm running." (wildly churn arms as if running)

12. Say with your fingertips, "This potato is hot!" (touch imaginary potato, jerk away from it)

13. Say with your nose, "I smell fresh pie." (sniff in appreciation)

14. Say with your chest, "I'm relaxed." (take a deep, relaxing breath)

15. Say with your legs, "I'm slipping!" (slip, but catch yourself before falling)

YOU ARE!

Players should now have some idea how easy it is to express themselves without using their voice. Further encourage their understanding by having them pantomime these situations wordlessly.

1. You are *happy* while playing catch.
2. You are *hungry* for lunch.
3. You are *surprised* at receiving a birthday present.
4. You are *sad* after dropping a glass.
5. You are *tired* after playing hard.
6. You are *puzzled* over a strange sound.
7. You are *cheerful* as you sweep the floor.
8. You are *peaceful* as you see the blue sky.
9. You are *not interested* in a television program.
10. You are *wondering* at your dog's disappearance.
11. You are *sleepy* as you go to bed.
12. You are *cold* as you stand in the snow.
13. You are *hot* as you stand in the sun.
14. You are *gay* as you hear peppy music.
15. You are *excited* over a ball game.

11

HANDY PANTOMIMES

Players may now be assigned their first simple, individual pantomimes (really charades). Each player performs one of the listed actions while the others try to guess what is being done. Although hands and arms are the principal means of expression other faculties should also be used. The purpose of this first performance is *clarity of action*. The leader should explain that even though the players know what they are doing, they must also make the action clear to the viewers. It contributes to clarity to have players briefly bow their heads just before and just after their performances; otherwise the viewers will think that the exits and entrances are part of the act.

1. Paste stamp on letter.
2. Open and close door.
3. Pick up and dial telephone.
4. Feed crumbs to birds.
5. Sail a glider.
6. Cut paper with scissors.
7. Clean a window.
8. Trim a hedge with large shears.

9. Open drawer, remove object, close drawer.
10. Play marbles.
11. Balance a stick on palm.
12. Place sheet in typewriter and type.
13. Take books from shelf, replace them.
14. Play a piano.
15. Fill glass from pitcher or faucet, drink.
16. Pick up and pet cat.
17. Hang a picture on wall.
18. Unscrew light bulb, replace it with new one.
19. Wind up and toss a toy top.
20. Select key from ring, unlock door.
21. Attach flag to rope, raise it.
22. Set nail on box, hammer it in.
23. Polish both shoes.
24. Take coins from pocket, count and replace them.
25. Wrap a package.
26. Adjust a television picture.
27. Catch and reel in a fish.
28. Dab brush in paint, paint a picture.
29. Lower bucket into a well, pull it up.
30. Briefly read several pages of a newspaper.
31. Pick up telescope, peer in several directions.
32. Play a trombone.
33. Pick up rug, shake and replace it.
34. Slice cake, eat a piece.
35. Trim a tree with Christmas ornaments.
36. Set a dinner table.
37. Sharpen a pencil, write.
38. Hang clothes on line.
39. Fly a kite, pull it in all the way.
40. Place saddle and bridle on a horse.

GOING PLACES

As a player crosses the stage he reveals that he is going to a particular place. He does this in either of two ways: by actions and attitudes which are in keeping with his destination, or by wearing or carrying an object which is associated with his destination. For instance, a player going to bed could sleepily rub his eyes or carry a clock.

The narrator may introduce a series of stunts by saying: "We are about to see a number of folks who are going places. Let's try to find out where they are going." Players may then cross the stage one after another with only a brief pause between each. As soon as a player exits the narrator might say something like: "That was Sleepyhead Sam—looks like *he's* going to *bed*."

Players can work out their own destinations or use the listed ones.

1. to bed (sleepily carry clock)
2. to work (briskly carry brief case)
3. to the beach (gaily bounce beach ball)
4. to a wedding (mischievously open box of rice)
5. to a picnic (bouncily carry picnic basket)
6. to a fire (quickly drag hose)
7. to school (happily carry books)
8. to church (solemnly carry prayer book)
9. to a party (humorously wear comic hat)
10. to dinner (hungrily carry fork)

PANTOMIME MARCH

This march takes place without any of the marchers' moving far from the spot. As the directions are given by the leader, the marchers move their legs up and down, turning as directed, but never going more than a few feet from the assigned spot.

Short and simple routines will be best for younger players, while older ones may work out longer and more complex movements. With a bit of practice this can be an unusually effective stunt—with or without accompanying music.

Here are a few ideas for marching which will get the group off to a fine start.

1. March in step
2. High step
3. Left foot only
4. Right foot only
5. Left turn
6. Right turn
7. About face
8. March on every other beat
9. Stand at attention
10. Clap in rhythm
11. Salute audience
12. Alternate marchers turn right, salute
13. Other alternate marchers turn left, face partner, salute
14. Swing arms
15. March in little circles
16. March in one-step squares
17. Dip knees every third step
18. Alternate marchers circle partners
19. Single line facing audience
20. Exit holding salute to audience

PANTOMIME ANSWERS

A player secretly thinks of an object of any kind. He then stands before the guessers and answers their questions about the object—not out loud, but with pantomime movements. The questions need not necessarily be of the kind that can be answered with a *yes* or *no*; the audience can ask any question which the actor can answer with a pantomime movement. Here is how the questions and answers might go if the actor's secret object were a *merry-go-round*.

"Is it large or small?" (player holds his hands out wide)

"Is it found in the house?" (player shakes head)

"Does it have moving parts?" (player nods)

"How does it move?" (player spins forefinger in flat circle)

"Does it carry things?" (player nods)

"What does it carry?" (player indicates audience and himself)

"Is it a bus?" (player shakes head)

"Where is it usually located?" (player gestures in several directions)

"Is it used for amusement?" (player nods)

"Is it a merry-go-round?" (player nods)

If desired, the audience may be required to guess the object within twenty questions.

YES AND NO PANTOMIMES

The game leader asks a series of questions on a level with the knowledge of the players. (See samples below.) The questions should be of the kind that can be answered either *yes* or *no*. Before each question the leader gives instructions, such as, "If the answer is *yes*, raise your left arm; if the answer is *no*, do nothing," or, "If the answer is *yes*, pat your head; if the answer is *no*, do nothing." A different movement should be requested with each question. Players must answer questions quickly without stopping to puzzle out the answer. If a player acts when he should do nothing, or if he does nothing when he should act, he drops out of the play. The final player wins the stunt. Sample questions:

1. Is the dime smaller than a nickel? (yes)
2. Does the sun rise in the west? (no)
3. Is *d* the third letter of the alphabet? (no)
4. Is Nevada one of our fifty states? (yes)
5. Is *re* a higher note than *do*? (yes)

ADD AND ACT

Here is pantomime fun for the entire group. The play leader starts things off by making a movement of any kind, such as shaking his left knee. The group must imitate the movement. The leader then makes a second motion, perhaps that of nodding his head. The group then performs both movements in order. The leader continues new actions without repeating those that went before, and the players must add the new action to the series. The fun lasts for as long as players can remember the actions in the right order, beginning with the first one.

MOVING AROUND

Each performer is allowed about one minute in which to move around in a circle in as many different ways as possible. For instance, a player might skip, stumble, run. The player with the cleverest performance might be awarded a prize. The instructor can assist his group to get the idea by reading aloud the following types of movement: skip, stumble, run, fall, trip, walk slow motion, slide, dance, tiptoe, stamp, hop, leap, jump backward, side-step, waddle, walk ape-like, walk stiff-legged, walk heel-to-toe, crawl on hands and knees.

CHALLENGES

Here is a stunt which helps actors to think quickly. Four or five volunteers sit on the stage. Members of the audience think up a pantomime act and challenge a volunteer to perform it. The challenges should not be too difficult. A volunteer might be asked to imitate an animal or to show how a policeman directs traffic. The audience may call for a single performer or for several actors to perform at once.

LAUGH ACT

The actor who performs this pantomime has but one thing to do—to laugh silently in as many ways as he can. The performer comes on stage, faces the audience, and takes a piece of paper from his pocket on which a joke is supposed to be written. He pretends to read the joke—and starts laughing at it! A clever actor can make the audience howl with delight by going through hilarious actions. Build up the laugh from a chuckle to a belly laugh and finish by collapsing from merriment, rolling on the floor, kicking your legs, drying your eyes or wringing out your handkerchief. The champion performer is one whose audience laughs more than he does!

DESCRIPTIONS

In this pantomime game, a player is to describe a famous person from history or fiction by one distinguishing characteristic. The viewers first try to guess the symbol of the pantomime (such as *tallness*) and then try to name the famous person who matches the description (such as *tall Abraham Lincoln*). Viewers may supply the name of any famous person who matches the description, not necessarily the example supplied below.

The group may use these examples for thinking up their own descriptions.

1. A tall man. (Abraham Lincoln)
2. A soldier. (George Washington)
3. A sleepy man. (Rip Van Winkle)
4. An orator. (Patrick Henry)
5. A small man. (Napoleon)
6. A writer. (William Shakespeare)
7. A detective. (Sherlock Holmes)
8. A singer. (Jenny Lind)
9. A king. (King Arthur)
10. A strong man. (Samson)

MUSICAL MOODS

Select a phonograph record (preferably a symphony) which includes several changes of mood and pace. Work out panto-mime movements that are in accord with the various moods. For example:

1. *Opening mood:* sit or lie about while reading, studying, quietly chatting.

2. *Awakening mood:* stand, stretch, look about for something active to do.

3. *Lively mood:* race about, play tag, laugh, shout.

4. *Restful mood:* grow tired, rub eyes, stretch, again lie down.

5. *Majestic mood:* march about in step, exit.

For other types of music, other actions are appropriate. Try to suit your movements to the rhythm and mood, to show that you understand the music.

ALL KINDS OF SONGS

A player pantomimes the act of singing a certain type of song. He does everything he can to express silently the nature and the mood of his song. The stage properties may be real or imaginary, though in most cases they should be imaginary. The type of song may be announced beforehand to the viewers, or they may try to guess it.

1. Patriotic song (wave flag, express appreciation of countryside).

2. Love song (sing tenderly, kneel as if serenading sweetheart, smile affectionately).

3. Indian song (whoop by clapping palm against mouth, dance in Indian fashion).

4. Sad song (sing slowly, weep, sadly gesture).

5. Cowboy song (sit astride chair as if riding horse, juggle reins about, twirl a rope).

6. Operatic song (sing grandly with deep dramatic expression in imitation of an opera singer).

7. Comic song (leap about, grin, gaily gesture).

8. Sea song (steer ship, imitate a sailor).

9. Lullaby (rock baby in arms, gently sway, sing softly).

10. Christmas song (imitate Santa Claus, pretend to decorate Christmas tree).

11. Military song (march, salute, stand at attention).

12. Sacred song (hold hymn book with both hands, sing reverently, bow head).

13. Hawaiian song (imitate Hawaiian dancer).

14. Winter song (skate on ice, throw snowballs).

15. Spanish song (imitate Spanish dancer, play guitar).

STRANGE SPEECHES

This is always good for lots of fun. A player merely pantomimes the act of giving a rousing speech. The more bounce and enthusiasm he puts into his act the better! He should make all sorts of wild gestures and exaggerated facial expressions.

A performer should be given a brief spoken introduction, such as, "And here is Jerry Wilson who will speak on the topic, *How to Fly a Kite in a Closet*." The pantomimed actions need have little or nothing to do with the announced topic. A prize might be awarded to the best—that is, to the most enthusiastic—performer. Players may think up their own topics or may select a listed one.

1. How to Fly a Kite in a Closet
2. My Cold Trip to the North Pole
3. What I Think About Spaghetti
4. How to Stand on Your Head
5. Famous Cowboys of the West
6. Washing Dishes Can Be Fun
7. How to Blow Soap Bubbles
8. Why I Like to Climb Trees
9. Build Your Own Airplane
10. Strange Facts about Alligators
11. How to Make a Cabbage Salad
12. What Happened on My Last Birthday
13. The Funniest Story I Ever Heard
14. Keep an Elephant for a Pet
15. How to Carry Peanut Butter in Your Pocket

ANIMAL ACTIONS

Players are secretly assigned the names of animals. In turn they act out the characteristic movements of these animals while the other players try to identify them. Players should be reminded that they may act out the sounds—such as the barking of a dog or the roaring of a lion—but they must do so in silence.

The listed animals (with suggested actions) are especially suitable for this stunt.

1. tiger (pace, growl)
2. beaver (swim, chew imaginary tree)
3. monkey (leap, scratch)
4. horse (gallop, buck)
5. bear (waddle, hug)
6. rabbit (hop, munch)
7. goat (charge, ram)
8. lion (roar, claw)
9. dog (bark, sit up)
10. kangaroo (hold limp paws, hop)
11. squirrel (dart, crack nuts)
12. seal (swim, flap fins)
13. wolf (howl, slink)
14. crocodile (swim, snap teeth)
15. gorilla (strut, beat chest)
16. bull (snort, paw ground)
17. cat (lap milk, curl up)
18. deer (tilt head, race lightly off)

BUY IT!

A player pantomimes the act of buying something. With a little thought, you can create a funny act, for example, by testing the product, dropping it, losing it, and so on. The player who buys perfume could sniff in joy, apply it to her elbows, drink it, pour it on her head, and so on.

Players should be allowed at least a few minutes to work out their acts. They should be announced something like, "Let's watch Miss Lucy Parker as she buys a bottle of perfume." Here are some items that will be interesting to purchase:

1. typewriter
2. tall lamp
3. gasoline-powered lawn-mower
4. bicycle
5. trombone
6. television set
7. derby hat
8. alarm clock
9. dictionary
10. oil painting
11. small automobile
12. long gloves
13. umbrella or parasol
14. toothbrush
15. automobile tire
16. portable sewing machine
17. set of dishes
18. diamond necklace
19. tank-type vacuum cleaner
20. evening gown
21. house paint
22. bouquet (corsage)
23. bathroom scale
24. riding boots
25. perfume
26. roller skates
27. basketball
28. fishing pole
29. earrings
30. garden hose

ACT-OUT STORIES

Two players perform this stunt together. One of them takes the part of the narrator, while the other is the actor. As they stand side by side onstage, the narrator tells (or reads) any kind of story, perhaps a children's classic such as "Jack and the Beanstalk" or a familiar poem which has lots of action. The narrator pauses every so often during the story to permit the player to act out an incident in pantomime.

The story then resumes until the next good place for the player to demonstrate the narrator's lines. The actor can make any kind of movement which illustrates the story, such as leaping about, putting on a pained expression, and performing specific acts such as climbing or sleeping. An offstage phonograph record playing suitable music will add much to the dramatic effect.

Another way of playing is to have the narrator tell a funny or embarrassing experience which is acted out by his partner. An entire show can be presented with this idea. Allow several couples time to prepare act-out stories, which can be offered at intervals during the party.

OCCUPATIONS

It would be a good idea to read aloud the listed occupations and permit each player to select the one he prefers. The more an occupation appeals to a player the more likely he is to succeed with it.

After everyone has given a solo pantomime, the leader may combine various players who can then work out a simple pantomime skit. Example: (a) The *airplane pilot* lands his craft in the field of the *farmer*. (b) The *farmer* telephones the *automobile mechanic* who repairs the plane. (c) The *mailman* enters and requests a ride from the *pilot*. (d) The *mailman* and the *pilot* take off together as the *farmer* and *automobile mechanic* wave good-by.

1. fireman
2. dressmaker
3. truck driver
4. automobile mechanic
5. jeweler
6. teacher
7. farmer
8. telephone operator
9. hairdresser
10. lawyer
11. carpenter
12. plumber
13. artist
14. judge
15. banker
16. musician
17. doctor
18. librarian
19. typist
20. gardener
21. nurse
22. bus driver
23. barber
24. mailman
25. butcher
26. saleslady
27. electrician
28. grocery checker
29. waiter
30. postal clerk
31. airplane pilot
32. painter
33. florist
34. cook
35. scientist
36. soldier
37. sailor
38. surveyor

39. printer
40. tailor
41. train engineer
42. usher
43. photographer
44. editor
45. dancer
46. magician
47. weatherman
48. maid
49. tourist guide

50. druggist
51. miner
52. candy maker
53. auctioneer
54. roofer
55. actor
56. songwriter
57. ticket seller
58. fashion model
59. shoemaker
60. athletic coach

TRAVELLERS

A player pantomimes the act of travelling in a particular manner and the audience tries to guess the method of travel. There are many ways in which an actor can reveal his means of transportation. For instance, the man on elephant-back could dismount and feed a peanut to the elephant, the man on a raft could push himself along with a pole, while the man in the covered wagon could peer out through the canvas while bumping up and down.

1. elephant-back
2. raft
3. covered wagon
4. tractor
5. motorized lawn mower
6. diving bell
7. roller coaster
8. helicopter
9. camel-back
10. elevator
11. speedboat
12. dog sled
13. ski lift
14. merry-go-round
15. basket of balloons

VOICE SOUNDS

This stunt is not only lots of fun but excellent practice for pantomimists. A performer pantomimes the act of making a vocal sound. He does not actually utter the sound, of course, but makes facial expressions and body movements which indicate it. The other players try to identify the sound he is making. After each player has performed, the teacher may make suggestions for improvement. The performer should be reminded that inasmuch as viewers cannot *hear* the sound, it must be revealed to them by means of *sight*. This can be accomplished through exaggerating the movements that we normally make with the sound.

1. sigh
2. sneeze
3. whistle
4. choke
5. shriek
6. growl
7. shout
8. laugh
9. breathe
10. sing
11. cough
12. smack
13. gulp
14. swallow
15. blow
16. whisper
17. gurgle
18. snore
19. hum
20. snarl
21. sniff
22. chuckle
23. cry
24. groan
25. pant
26. gasp
27. giggle
28. snort
29. bark
30. sputter

ALL SORTS OF SOUNDS

Here is another fine stunt with sounds. A player goes through the pantomimed act of producing a noise. Examples: for *tinkle* he might pretend to tap a spoon against a drinking glass, for *drip* he might turn off a faucet and cup his hand to hear the remaining drops, for *flutter* he might raise a flag and then listen to its motions in the wind.

1. tinkle
2. drip
3. flutter
4. pound
5. slide
6. clap
7. rip
8. scratch
9. boom
10. crack
11. shuffle
12. skid
13. slam
14. shatter
15. chop
16. ring
17. knock
18. zoom
19. crash
20. break
21. tap
22. scrape
23. crackle
24. cut
25. rub
26. bounce
27. pop
28. squeak
29. roll
30. blast

WHAT GAME AM I PLAYING?

Each player is assigned a game or sport. He reveals it by acting it out in pantomime. The following games will serve.

1. golf
2. skating
3. soccer
4. long-distance run
5. tennis
6. high jump
7. basketball
8. croquet
9. water ski
10. football
11. broad jump
12. baseball
13. bowling
14. archery
15. badminton
16. handball
17. hurdle race
18. sprint
19. volley ball
20. speedboat race
21. ice hockey
22. javelin throw
23. skiing
24. table tennis
25. pole vault
26. discus throw
27. weight lifting
28. shot-put
29. dart throw
30. dodge ball

PANTOMIME PARADE

Players enter and exit one after another while pantomiming persons and animals which might be seen in or around a parade. Peppy music might be played in the background. An announcer might name the character as the actor reaches the middle of the stage. Here are suggested entries in your pantomime parade:

1. parade marshal
2. drum major, majorette
3. musicians
4. horses
5. trick dog and master
6. clowns, comics
7. dancers
8. policeman
9. popcorn and peanut salesmen
10. balloon salesmen
11. animal mascots and masters
12. local heroes and leading citizens
13. soldiers, sailors, airmen
14. Boy Scouts, Girl Scouts
15. sign carriers
16. elves, goblins, ghosts
17. athletes
18. cowboys
19. Indians
20. dragons
21. stunt marchers
22. beauty queens
23. organ grinder and monkey
24. magician
25. folks with exhibits and displays

WHERE AM I?

This stunt is excellent for beginners, but just as much fun for advanced actors and actresses. A player selects one of the listed locations and tries to reveal where he is to the audience through pantomime performance. The act may be serious or comical, or perhaps a mixture of both.

1. in a submarine
2. on a roof
3. in a gold mine
4. on parade
5. in a jewelry store
6. in a bank
7. in a zoo
8. in a printing shop
9. in a lighthouse
10. in a theatre
11. on a train
12. in a café
13. in a museum
14. in a library
15. in a fire station
16. on shipboard
17. up an apple tree
18. in a kitchen
19. in a courtroom
20. in the hospital
21. on a picnic
22. in the desert
23. on a space ship
24. in an aquarium
25. in a closet
26. in a shoe shop
27. in a taxi
28. behind a ticket booth
29. in a canoe
30. on a mountaintop

LIVING SONGS

A narrator reads aloud the words of a well-known song while two or more pantomimists in turn act out the title as a whole. Music can accompany the words and actions. By making the most of the words a group can offer a lively performance. The listed songs and ballads are especially suitable for this stunt.

1. For He's a Jolly Good Fellow
2. My Bonnie
3. When Johnny Comes Marching Home
4. Good-By, My Lover, Good-By
5. Home, Sweet Home
6. Jeanie with the Light Brown Hair
7. Tramp, Tramp, Tramp
8. Sailing
9. The Old Oaken Bucket
10. Oh, Susanna
11. Row, Row, Row Your Boat
12. Good Night, Ladies
13. Home on the Range
14. Oh, My Darling Clementine
15. Pop! Goes the Weasel

DIZZY DINNERS

This pantomime usually gets lots of laughs, but real "props" are needed for greatest fun. The player goes through the motions of mixing an odd dish for dinner. The principal idea is for the pantomimist to drop all sorts of strange and funny items into a mixing bowl. Here are some suggestions:

1. Peel a potato, add the peels, throw potato over shoulder.

2. Take catsup bottle, unscrew cap, shake catsup into bowl, taste mixture, decide more catsup is needed, repeat action with two or three more bottles.

3. Grab a handful of the mixture, lick it, happily nod, pour in the contents of a small box, shrug, add box also.

4. Pick up newspaper, turn pages, briefly read, tear paper into shreds, let them flutter into bowl.

5. Look around for something else to add, notice button on coat, jerk it off, chop it up, add to bowl.

6. Crack several eggs over bowl, also toss shells into it.

7. Look around for something else to add, sweep floor, pour sweepings into bowl.

8. Pick up sugar bowl, taste sugar, smile at its sweetness, add several handfuls of sugar, taste mixture, painfully choke and fall.

Charades

Charades is a fun-filled game in which a word or a series of words is acted out in pantomime for the audience to guess. The charade maker reveals his secret word in any way he can— by motioning or gesturing or posing. All his actions are done in silence; no words are spoken, nor does he form words with his lips.

For example: a player could reveal the first part of the word *watermelon* by pretending to pour and drink a glass of water. The viewers might guess wrong at first by asking if he means *glass* or *drink*. When the actor shakes his head they keep guessing until they discover that he means *water*. The actor could then reveal the second part of the word (or the word as a whole) by pretending to slice and eat a piece of melon.

If a single word (rather than a whole sentence) is to be guessed, you would first hold up the number of fingers equal to the number of syllables in your secret word. The word *rainbow*, for instance, contains two syllables, so you would hold up two fingers to let the audience know this. You next hold up one finger to indicate that you will now act out the first syllable. When they have guessed *rain*, you hold up two fingers to show that you will next act out the second syllable.

If the charade consists of a whole sentence you would hold up as many fingers as there are words in your sentence. If the audience fails to guess the first word you can hold up two fingers to show them that you will go on to the second word. You can later come back to the first word if necessary.

To indicate small words in a sentence, hold your thumb and forefinger about one inch apart. This will help the audience to guess such small words as *the, it, and, or.*

You need only reveal the *sound* of your secret word or syllable, not necessarily its correct spelling. So if you wish to reveal the word *right*, you could pretend to *write*. Let the audience know that you are giving them a word which rhymes with your secret word by first cupping your hand to your ear. This lets them know that the secret word *sounds like* the word that you want them to guess. You can then indicate an object which rhymes with your secret word. For the sound of *sea*, for example, you would give the audience a hint that it rhymes with *knee* by pointing to your knee.

A game of charades usually consists of words with two syllables or more; however, words with just one syllable add variety to the play. Beginners may wish to act out one-syllable words such as *tree, look, spin.*

The game may be played with teams or simply with individual performers. For team play, one side acts out several charades (one at a time) for the other side to guess. An umpire with a watch with a second-hand keeps time. The team completing its charades in the fewer number of minutes wins the game. For individual play, any volunteer may give several charades for the group to guess.

A time limit of three minutes may be set in advance for the discovery of a difficult secret word or sentence. Or, you may prefer to play as long as it takes for the sentence to be guessed.

A B C CHARADES

Each player is assigned a different letter of the alphabet. He is allowed one minute in which to act out as many objects as possible which begin with his letter. The performer having the letter *A* might act out *apple, arm, automobile, ape, airplane.* When the viewers guess an object the performer scores a point. The player with the most points at the end of the game wins. If desired, a shorter or longer performance period may be set.

THREE-LETTER CHARADES

This is played somewhat as the above game, except that players try to act out as many objects as possible which are spelled with three letters. A player might try *cat, ice, cup, rug, hoe.*

After a number of three-letter words, you might try four-letter or five-letter words.

FACTS ABOUT FOLKS

Before playing this game the leader collects one interesting secret fact about everyone in the room. He then says something like "And here is something interesting about Tommy Carter." An assigned player then acts out the secret fact, while the rest of the players try to guess what the secret is. Here are typical facts which might be used.

1. He was born in Nebraska.
2. She has three older brothers.
3. His favorite sport is swimming.
4. Her middle name is Belle.
5. His hobby is photography.

WHAT'S IN THE NEWS?

A few players pretend to read a newspaper heading, then together act out for the rest of the players or audience the event which they have "read." The audience need only guess the general nature of the headline. Players may select their own topics or use the following headings:

1. Students Honored at Graduation
2. Voters Flock to Polls
3. Rocket Fired toward Moon
4. Relay Team Sets Track Record
5. Storm Hits City
6. Fireworks Displayed on Independence Day
7. Bathers Crowd Cool Beaches
8. Wedding Plans Revealed
9. General Reviews Troops
10. Hikers Explore Desert

CHARADE NUMBERS

The idea of this game is for a player to act out a word which is connected with a number. The viewers silently guess the word from which they guess aloud the number. For example, if the actor portrayed the word *alphabet* the audience would guess number 26—the number of letters in the alphabet. In this list of usable words and numbers, the charade words are in italics.

1. 7 days in a *week*.
2. 4 *seasons*.
3. 3 corners to a *triangle*.
4. 60 seconds to a *minute*.
5. 10 *fingers* on hands.
6. 24 hours to a *day*.
7. 31 days in *March*.
8. 9 *planets*.
9. 2 *ears* on a person's head.
10. 12 months in a *year*.

WHO AM I?

Half the players leave the room. They then return, one at a
time, as fully disguised as possible. (A typical disguise might
be an oversized coat, plus a paper sack—cut with eye-holes—
over the head.) The actor performs any kind of a pantomime
which will reveal his real identity. For instance, a boy who is
known to have a paper route might pretend to deliver papers;
a girl who plays a musical instrument might imitate a musician.
The clues should not be too easy.

When all the members of one group have been identified,
they become the guessers of the other group.

DOG NAMES

Here is a charade with a humorous twist. A player acts out
the name of his dog. However, his dog does not have a commonplace name such as Fido or Rover, but the strangest
name possible. He might be called Bonechew or Barkerboy or
Catchase. It is up to the audience to discover the unusual name.

MYSTERY CHARADES

This game has a mysterious ending to it. The charade actor thinks of some action which he wants the viewers to perform. His whole charade-sentence then tells them exactly what they must do. As soon as the viewers guess the charade-sentence, they must perform the action. The following suggestions will get the game off to a good start.

1. Clap your hands five times.
2. Imitate a monkey.
3. Shake hands with three friends.
4. Go to sleep.
5. Count aloud from ten back to one.
6. Walk stiff-legged in a circle.
7. Touch your right elbow to your right heel.
8. Compliment the person next to you.
9. Sing out loud.
10. Take off and replace your shoes.

NAME CHARADES

This one is fun for both beginners and experts. Below are lists of names of boys and girls which are especially good for charade play. The idea is to act out the sound of the first part of the name. This supplies the audience with a clue for guessing the complete name. The viewers should be informed in advance that they will be given only the first part of a name and that they must take it from there.

Girls	*Boys*
1. Lois (low)	1. Richard (rich)
2. Julia (jewel)	2. Gilbert (gill)
3. Lydia (lid)	3. John (jaw)
4. Mildred (mill)	4. Dennis (den)
5. Phyllis (fill)	5. Walter (wall)
6. Peggy (peg)	6. Woodrow (wood)
7. Patricia (pat)	7. Tony (toe)
8. Jane (jay)	8. Michael (my)
9. Doris (door)	9. Raymond (ray)
10. Grace (gray)	10. Donald (dawn)
11. Barbara (bar)	11. Orville (ore)
12. Sharon (share)	12. Cecil (see)
13. Gladys (glad)	13. Keith (key)
14. Sylvia (sill)	14. Lionel (lion)
15. Rose (row)	15. Chester (chest)
16. Sandra (sand)	16. David (day)
17. Harriet (hair)	17. Warren (war)
18. Joyce (joy)	18. Carl (car)
19. Irene (eye)	19. Eugene (you)
20. Hazel (hay)	20. Stuart (stew)

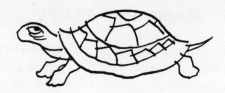

GUESS THE ANIMAL CHARADES

A player acts out a sentence that might be spoken by an animal or bird. The audience tries to guess both the sentence and the creature as soon as possible.

1. I like to nibble the top leaves (giraffe)
2. My picture is on money (eagle)
3. People say I move slowly (turtle)
4. Listen to me talk (parrot)
5. My big bill holds lots of fish (pelican)
6. Here comes that toreador (bull)
7. Watch my spout (whale)
8. I am a sly one (fox)
9. My arms are built for swinging (monkey)
10. I am a symbol of peace (dove)
11. Farmers try to scare me (crow)
12. I am also called a mountain lion (cougar)
13. Your coat may come from me (sheep)
14. I am large, white, and graceful (swan)
15. I live within sight of the pyramids (camel)

NAME THE STATE

The performer acts out a word or sound which forms only a part of the name of one of the 20 states listed below. The audience must guess the state from the acted-out portion.

1. Florida (floor)
2. Oklahoma (home)
3. Pennsylvania (pen)
4. Rhode Island (road)
5. Utah (you)
6. Delaware (wear)
7. Mississippi (sip)
8. Ohio (high)
9. Indiana (Indian)
10. Oregon (ore)
11. Maryland (merry)
12. North Dakota (coat)
13. California (four)
14. Nebraska (ask)
15. Washington (wash)
16. Connecticut (connect)
17. Colorado (call)
18. Missouri (miss)
19. Montana (tan)
20. Tennessee (ten)

CHANCE CHARADES

This one will help actors and actresses to think and act quickly while onstage. A player goes onstage where an assistant holds an open book before him. (It can be any page of any book.) The player closes his eyes and jabs a finger onto the page. He then acts out whatever word his finger lands upon. He takes three turns at poking and acting. Some of the words will be easy and others will be difficult, but all will help the player to become a better performer.

CHARADES ON SPECIAL SUBJECTS

Thinking up charades is often more difficult than acting them out. Here are handy lists of special topics to consult when you are stumped for an idea. The charade maker should indicate the category by gestures before acting. For instance, with *Precious Stones and Gems*, you might indicate a pendant on a necklace or a ring on your finger, until the audience guesses that the category is "jewel." Then each word should be split into syllables if the whole word is too difficult for the audience to guess. Take "opal"—split into an exclamation "oh" and a friend "pal."

Precious Stones and Gems

1. emerald
2. opal
3. diamond
4. sapphire
5. agate
6. amethyst
7. onyx
8. ruby
9. pearl
10. topaz
11. garnet
12. turquoise

Musical Instruments

1. clarinet
2. trombone
3. drum
4. harp
5. violin
6. flute
7. trumpet
8. piccolo
9. piano
10. tuba
11. organ
12. saxophone

Birds

1. oriole
2. swallow
3. bluebird
4. owl
5. eagle
6. wren
7. parakeet
8. sparrow
9. turkey
10. hawk
11. penguin
12. dove
13. cardinal
14. lark
15. duck
16. canary
17. robin
18. parrot
19. blackbird
20. chicken
21. raven
22. ostrich
23. goose
24. crow
25. mockingbird
26. sea gull
27. pheasant
28. pigeon
29. woodpecker
30. hummingbird
31. quail
32. swan
33. goldfinch
34. chickadee
35. stork
36. nightingale
37. thrush
38. crane
39. falcon
40. albatross

Fish

1. mackerel
2. bass
3. perch
4. salmon
5. sailfish
6. barracuda
7. trout
8. sardine
9. cod
10. shark
11. tuna
12. swordfish

Berries and Nuts

1. loganberry
2. almond
3. filbert
4. blueberry
5. coconut
6. strawberry
7. cashew
8. blackberry
9. cranberry
10. pecan
11. gooseberry
12. peanut
13. raspberry
14. mulberry
15. walnut
16. Brazil nut

Vegetables

1. carrot
2. spinach
3. celery
4. beet
5. lettuce
6. squash
7. artichoke
8. onion
9. potato
10. turnip
11. radish
12. garlic
13. corn
14. parsnip
15. cabbage
16. bean
17. tomato
18. pumpkin
19. peas
20. broccoli
21. asparagus
22. cauliflower
23. parsley
24. cucumber
25. pepper
26. eggplant
27. yam
28. horse-radish
29. rhubarb
30. okra

Fruits

1. peach
2. cherry
3. pineapple
4. apple
5. grape
6. watermelon
7. plum
8. orange
9. apricot
10. lime
11. pear
12. banana
13. fig
14. cantaloupe
15. grapefruit
16. pomegranate
17. date
18. lemon
19. persimmon
20. quince
21. nectarine
22. prune
23. crab apple
24. tangerine

Flowers

1. tulip
2. poppy
3. zinnia
4. carnation
5. lily
6. iris
7. rose
8. pansy
9. snapdragon
10. orchid
11. petunia
12. violet
13. lilac
14. daisy
15. chrysanthemum
16. hibiscus
17. cosmos
18. geranium
19. sunflower
20. daffodil

Trees

1. maple
2. cypress
3. oak
4. birch
5. willow
6. redwood
7. hemlock
8. fir
9. beech
10. cottonwood
11. elm
12. ash
13. cedar
14. palm
15. sycamore
16. pine
17. spruce
18. balsam
19. poplar
20. magnolia

Planets

1. Venus
2. Neptune
3. Mars
4. Earth
5. Jupiter
6. Mercury
7. Pluto
8. Saturn
9. Uranus

Foreign Countries

1. Brazil
2. Australia
3. Turkey
4. India
5. Panama
6. Holland
7. Japan
8. Portugal
9. Russia
10. Peru
11. China
12. Belgium
13. Sweden
14. Mexico
15. Spain
16. Denmark
17. Egypt
18. Norway
19. Pakistan
20. Chile
21. Italy
22. Greece
23. France
24. Argentina

LEAN
GREEN

RHYMING WORD CHARADES

Each player in turn is assigned one of the secret words listed below. Before the performer begins, the audience is told that the word suggested by the pantomimed action rhymes with the secret word. The idea is to guess both words. For instance, if the pantomimist pretends to saw a piece of wood the viewers would first have to guess the word *saw*. The players in the audience may shout as many guesses as they can as rapidly as they can. When a guesser shouts the word *saw*, the pantomimist nods to indicate that he has found the right word. The viewers now try to guess the secret word which rhymes with *saw*, which might be *law*.

This stunt is especially good for team play. Members of each team take turns performing while the other team guesses. The team ending with the greater number of secret words is the winner. Here are some secret words with suggestions for pantomiming them.

1. cake (pretend to *shake* hands)
2. gold (shiver as if *cold*)
3. ball (hold hand at *tall* level)
4. leap (pretend to *sleep*)
5. ring (pretend to *sing*)
6. cook (pretend to read *book*)
7. sound (*pound* fist)
8. out (cup hands, *shout*)
9. blue (hold up *two* fingers)
10. sink (*blink* your eyes or pretend to *drink*)
11. drop (*hop* around)
12. match (*scratch* arm)
13. green (*lean* to one side)
14. toe (pretend to *row* boat)
15. ice (pretend to *slice* bread)
16. chair (pat *hair*)
17. burn (*turn* around in circle)
18. fine (pretend to *shine* shoes)
19. bush (*push* away)
20. calm (point to *palm*)
21. chance (*dance* about)
22. please (tightly *squeeze* arm)
23. ripe (pretend to *type*)
24. snow (pretend to *sew*)
25. haste (pretend to *taste*)

MILLION DOLLAR CHARADES

What would you say if you were offered a million dollars?
Everyone playing this game has an opportunity to act out in
pantomime what he would reply if someone walked up and
offered to give him a million dollars. The other players try
to guess what the pantomimist is saying. Performers should
try to be as funny and clever as possible. You may act out the
listed replies, or you may prefer to think up your own.

1. I think I'm going to faint.
2. Just stuff it in my pocket.
3. Thank you; call again.
4. I must be dreaming.
5. I'll spend it all on candy.
6. Please repeat that.
7. That's a funny joke.
8. That's the best offer I've had this week.
9. Quit your kidding.
10. Sorry, I'm not interested.
11. I wouldn't know what to do with it.
12. I'm speechless.
13. I'll think it over.
14. Give it to someone else.
15. I already have a million dollars.

HINK-PINK CHARADES

Each player is assigned to act out for the audience to guess two single syllable words which complete a little but not necessarily sensible rhyme. (More difficult would be "Hinky Pinky" Charades—two rhyming words of two syllables each. Advanced players could try that.)

1. long song
2. small ball
3. pull wool
4. flat hat
5. my pie
6. keep sheep
7. hurl pearl
8. slow throw
9. fly high
10. red head
11. sweet wheat
12. warm storm
13. crush mush
14. I spy
15. shun sun
16. whole bowl
17. stop mop
18. see bee
19. grip lip
20. jump stump
21. munch lunch
22. scrub tub
23. love dove
24. sad lad
25. bake cake
26. blue shoe
27. clean screen
28. big fig
29. spill pill
30. house mouse
31. float boat
32. brown clown
33. sock clock
34. one gun
35. tug rug
36. throw snow
37. drink ink
38. chew stew
39. sour flower
40. toss sauce

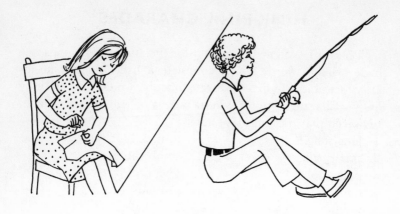

TOMORROW'S TASK

Players take turns in revealing in pantomime something which they are going to do tomorrow. The audience should be told in advance that each task is described in just two words and that both words start with the same letter.

1. sell sardines
2. repair roof
3. bake biscuits
4. sew socks
5. chase chipmunks
6. taste turnips
7. polish piano
8. wash windows
9. dig diamonds
10. catch crocodiles
11. sharpen scissors
12. grow garlic
13. collect cash
14. fry fish
15. make masks

16. play piccolo
17. cook cabbage
18. tame tigers
19. find food
20. peel potatoes
21. clean closet
22. press pants
23. buy bananas
24. ride rhinoceros
25. pick peaches
26. feed foxes
27. carry coal
28. borrow book
29. sail sea
30. watch walruses

KING CHARADES

Players act out these words which end in *king*. Viewers try to guess which kind of king is on the throne, or rather on the stage.

1. waking
2. parking
3. shrieking
4. thinking
5. breaking
6. joking
7. hiking
8. packing
9. working
10. talking
11. cooking
12. sneaking
13. backing
14. choking
15. raking
16. locking
17. poking
18. peeking
19. honking
20. smacking
21. soaking
22. stacking
23. shaking
24. ducking
25. stroking
26. blocking
27. clicking
28. hacking
29. wrecking
30. kicking
31. quacking
32. blinking
33. basking
34. licking
35. thanking
36. tracking
37. sticking
38. tacking
39. sinking
40. striking

FORTY FAVORITE PROVERBS

Proverbs are always welcome guests at a charade party. The following selections are especially good for act-out fun.

1. Birds of a feather flock together.
2. He who laughs last laughs best.
3. Nothing ventured, nothing gained.
4. A word to the wise is sufficient.
5. We learn to do by doing.
6. Let sleeping dogs lie.
7. Half a loaf is better than none.
8. All things come to him who waits.
9. Haste makes waste.
10. Where there's smoke there's fire.
11. Every cloud has a silver lining.
12. Easy come, easy go.
13. A miss is as good as a mile.
14. It is never too late to learn.
15. Seeing is believing.
16. Don't count your chickens before they're hatched.
17. Actions speak louder than words.
18. Too many cooks spoil the broth.
19. A new broom sweeps clean.
20. Business before pleasure.
21. Better safe than sorry.
22. Two heads are better than one.
23. A bird in the hand is worth two in the bush.
24. Practice makes perfect.
25. A stitch in time saves nine.
26. Heaven helps those who help themselves.
27. Don't cry over spilt milk.
28. Absence makes the heart grow fonder.
29. Better late than never.

30. Paddle your own canoe.
31. Turn-about is fair play.
32. You can't have your cake and eat it too.
33. A rolling stone gathers no moss.
34. If at first you don't succeed, try, try again.
35. Practice what you preach.
36. Out of sight, out of mind.
37. A barking dog never bites.
38. A friend in need is a friend indeed.
39. A watched pot never boils.
40. A penny saved is a penny earned.

ADD-A-LETTER CHARADES

The pantomimist acts out a word, such as *tree*, which the viewers must guess. Once they have the sound of *tree*, they must add a single letter of the alphabet to reveal the secret word, while the actor tries to help them with gestures. In the case of *tree*, the proper letter to be added is T, thus making the secret word of *treat*. The sound (not the spelling) of the acted-out word, plus the sound of an added letter, completes the secret word.

1. treat (*tree* plus *T*)
2. single (*sing* plus *L*)
3. droop (*drew* plus *P*)
4. sticky (*stick* plus *E*)
5. tense (*ten* plus *S*)
6. ready (*red* plus *E*)
7. goat (*go* plus *T*)
8. short (*shore* plus *T*)

9. toot (*two* plus *T*)
10. slate (*sleigh* plus *T*)
11. yellow (*yell* plus *O*)
12. load (*low* plus *D*)
13. soak (*sew* plus *K*)
14. shine (*shy* plus *N*)
15. squawk (*squaw* plus *K*)
16. great (*gray* plus *T*)
17. hair (*hay* plus *R*)
18. arrow (*air* plus *O*)
19. cattle (*cat* plus *L*)
20. change (*chain* plus *G*)
21. slide (*sly* plus *D*)
22. cellar (*sell* plus *R*)
23. grope (*grow* plus *P*)
24. frenzy (*friend* plus *Z*)
25. pine (*pie* plus *N*)
26. hurry (*her* plus *E*)
27. hide (*high* plus *D*)
28. slipper (*slip* plus *R*)
29. spice (*spy* plus *S*)
30. storm (*store* plus *M*)

THE SOUND OF T

Players take turns in acting out the listed words. Even though the viewers are informed that all the words end with the sound of *t* they may have to do some extra thinking in order to come up with the right answers.

1. activity
2. celebrity
3. curiosity
4. hilarity
5. timidity
6. university
7. intensity
8. liberty
9. oddity
10. personality
11. mighty
12. captivity
13. poverty
14. piety
15. electricity
16. beauty
17. serenity
18. royalty
19. perplexity
20. thrifty
21. authority
22. deputy
23. stability
24. property
25. ability
26. velocity
27. popularity
28. immensity
29. rapidity
30. prosperity

GO-TOGETHER WORDS

Each player in turn acts out a word which is commonly matched with another word, such as *salt* which is usually associated with *pepper*. The audience must guess the go-together words.

1. salt and pepper
2. up and down
3. hammer and nail
4. wash and dry
5. read and write
6. sun and moon
7. ham and eggs
8. day and night
9. soap and water
10. work and play
11. cup and saucer
12. fast and slow
13. enter and exit
14. bow and arrow
15. long and short
16. dog and cat
17. bread and butter
18. lock and key
19. bat and ball
20. east and west
21. black and white
22. knife and fork
23. hook and line
24. pail and shovel
25. pen and pencil
26. nut and bolt
27. shoes and socks
28. see and hear
29. arms and legs
30. land and sea
31. king and queen
32. aim and fire
33. first and last
34. give and take
35. stop and go
36. eat and drink
37. win and lose
38. yes and no
39. rich and poor
40. add and subtract
41. heel and toe
42. bride and groom
43. buy and sell
44. boy and girl
45. thick and thin
46. high and low
47. push and pull
48. teacher and student
49. hat and coat
50. brush and comb

SYNONYM CHARADES

This is a charade game which requires a good knowledge of terminology. The pantomimists (either individuals taking turns or teams alternating), keeping the list secret, act out the listed words for an audience (or for the other team) to guess. When someone in the audience (or a member of the guessing team) thinks he knows the word being acted out, he must call out two words, synonyms (words meaning more or less the same thing) which should correspond to those on this list. However, it's best not to be too exact in the requirements, as there are many words meaning the same thing. For example, the list calls for *quick* and *fast*, but *rapid* and *speedy* would be just as acceptable. If the guess is wrong, the pantomimist continues until he hears two correct words. Then the game continues with the next synonyms.

1. quick and fast
2. laugh and chuckle
3. strong and mighty
4. look and see
5. mystery and puzzle
6. drop and spill
7. fasten and tie
8. listen and hear
9. sleep and slumber
10. tune and melody
11. small and tiny
12. far and distant
13. shy and timid
14. brave and courageous
15. shout and yell
16. calm and peaceful
17. rich and wealthy
18. wise and intelligent
19. groan and moan
20. breeze and wind
21. beautiful and attractive
22. gay and merry
23. sad and gloomy
24. disappear and vanish
25. late and tardy
26. price and cost
27. dinner and supper
28. love and affection
29. hard and solid
30. heavy and weighty
31. work and effort
32. grab and grasp
33. honest and truthful
34. easy and simple

35. take and receive
36. throw and toss
37. run and sprint
38. keep and save
39. stone and rock
40. valuable and precious
41. want and desire
42. trip and journey
43. repair and mend
44. thin and slim
45. friend and chum
46. woman and lady
47. thought and idea

48. begin and start
49. new and fresh
50. talk and speak
51. shake and shiver
52. city and town
53. large and giant
54. empty and vacant
55. choose and select
56. umpire and referee
57. street and avenue
58. meadow and field
59. gift and present
60. game and sport

ANTONYM CHARADES

This is played just like the preceding game, except that the guessers try to think of the word being acted out and another that means the opposite.

1. open and close
2. north and south
3. agree and oppose
4. confident and afraid
5. believe and doubt
6. continue and cease
7. active and still
8. bright and dull
9. fancy and plain
10. freedom and slavery
11. gentle and rough
12. silence and noise
13. happy and sorrowful
14. gain and loss
15. famous and unknown
16. hit and miss
17. proud and humble
18. dangerous and safe
19. scarce and abundant
20. few and many
21. over and under
22. different and same
23. deep and shallow
24. accept and reject
25. collect and scatter
26. crooked and straight
27. melt and freeze
28. top and bottom
29. equal and uneven
30. separate and join
31. dry and wet
32. interesting and boring
33. serious and funny
34. wrong and right
35. all and none
36. cloudy and clear
37. stand and sit
38. mountain and valley
39. winter and summer
40. follow and lead
41. in and out
42. perfect and faulty
43. thrifty and wasteful
44. strange and ordinary
45. ready and unprepared
46. sweet and sour
47. build and destroy
48. tight and loose
49. on and off
50. backward and forward
51. left and right
52. best and worst
53. true and false
54. inhale and exhale
55. float and sink
56. often and seldom

57. nothing and something
58. most and least
59. ask and answer
60. increase and decrease

WORDS WITH SIMILAR SPELLINGS

The following list contains pairs of words which are spelled the same but have different meanings. Two players act out the different meanings at the same time, for the viewers to guess.

1. park *car, recreational* park
2. palm *of hand,* palm *tree*
3. *dollar* bill, *bird's* bill
4. *printing* press, press *button*
5. tire *of work, auto* tire
6. stamp *foot, postage* stamp
7. spring *up, drink from* spring
8. *baseball* bat, *animal* bat
9. *eat* nut, *tighten* nut
10. loaf *of bread,* loaf *around*
11. pound *of apples,* pound *fist*
12. pine *tree,* pine *sorrowfully*
13. sink *in water, kitchen* sink
14. *eat* prune, prune *a bush*
15. rock *baby, throw* rock
16. *open* chest, *rub* chest
17. fly *away, swat* fly
18. trip *and fall, go on* trip
19. *eat* roll, roll *on floor*
20. *writing* pen, *pig* pen
21. ring *bell, finger* ring
22. seal *letter, the animal* seal
23. *garden* fence, fence *with a sword*

24. *baseball* pitcher, *flower* pitcher
25. duck *the head*, *quacking* duck
26. *toy* top, top *of head*
27. sock *on foot*, sock *a ball*
28. squash *a hat*, the *vegetable* squash
29. tug *a rope*, *harbor* tug
30. *electric* light, light *in weight*

FAMILIAR SIMILES

Here are fifty phrases which compare things—called similes. All of them are familiar to us and can be used for a rousing game of charades. As an actor pretends to flip pancakes the audience will catch on that the saying is *As flat as a pancake.*

1. As busy as a bee.
2. As red as a rose.
3. As quick as a wink.
4. As easy as pie.
5. As curious as a cat.
6. As pretty as a picture.
7. As fresh as a daisy.
8. As strong as an ox.
9. As slow as molasses.
10. As fit as a fiddle.
11. As hard as a rock.
12. As flat as a pancake.
13. As light as a feather.
14. As smooth as silk.
15. As stubborn as a mule.
16. As white as snow.
17. As tight as a drum.
18. As happy as a lark.

19. As dry as a bone.
20. As fast as lightning.
21. As slippery as an eel.
22. As good as gold.
23. As old as Methuselah.
24. As blind as a bat.
25. As pale as a ghost.
26. As snug as a bug in a rug.
27. As quiet as a mouse.
28. As clear as mud.
29. As swift as the wind.
30. As mad as a wet hen.
31. As black as coal.
32. As sharp as a tack.
33. As peaceful as a dove.
34. As hungry as a horse.
35. As green as grass.
36. As clean as a hound's tooth.
37. As stiff as a board.
38. As smart as a whip.
39. As silly as a goose.
40. As weak as a kitten.
41. As blue as the sky.
42. As fat as a pig.
43. As sticky as glue.
44. As sly as a fox.
45. As proud as a peacock.
46. As solid as an oak.
47. As neat as a pin.
48. As wise as an owl.
49. As cool as a cucumber.
50. As straight as an arrow.

WORDS WITH SIMILAR SOUNDS

Here is an opportunity for two pantomimists to perform side by side at the same time. Each acts out one of the paired words. Both words sound almost the same although they have different spellings and different meanings. As soon as the viewers guess one of the words they will quickly find the other. It will be interesting to see which performer helps the audience the most.

1. beat, beet
2. cot, caught
3. tea, tee
4. blue, blew
5. meat, meet
6. sun, son
7. hair, hare
8. Sunday, sundae
9. sew, sow
10. four, fore
11. rode, road
12. see, sea
13. eight, ate
14. brake, break
15. clothes, close
16. soar, sore
17. hour, our
18. I, eye
19. knight, night
20. sale, sail
21. pear, pair
22. one, won
23. cent, scent
24. horse, hoarse
25. write, right
26. plane, plain
27. tide, tied
28. ball, bawl
29. pail, pale
30. rap, wrap
31. waist, waste
32. heal, heel
33. him, hymn
34. toe, tow
35. beach, beech
36. wait, weight
37. pain, pane
38. stake, steak
39. buy, by
40. board, bored

ANAGRAM CHARADES

An anagram is a word built by rearranging the letters of another word. For this charade the exact letters in the first word are used to build the second word. For instance, from the word *swing* the anagram of *wings* could be built.

To begin, a player acts out the first word, and when this is guessed by one of the viewers, he (or his team) must rearrange its letters to find the secret word which contains the same letters. The first viewer (or team) to do this is awarded a point for himself (or for his team). If a blackboard is handy the game director can write out the first word (once it is guessed) so as to make it easier for viewers to rearrange its letters.

The first word in each of the following sets is the one to be acted out. The second word suggests an anagram answer, although in some cases there are several answers possible.

1. lamp (palm)
2. pear (reap)
3. stop (post)
4. read (dare)
5. stew (west)
6. eat (tea)
7. north (thorn)
8. petal (plate)
9. rope (pore)
10. sword (words)
11. taste (state)
12. throw (worth)
13. stab (bats)
14. race (care)
15. blow (bowl)
16. leap (peal)
17. grin (ring)
18. plum (lump)
19. tide (diet)
20. drop (prod)
21. shoe (hose)
22. golf (flog)
23. steam (meats)
24. wolf (flow)
25. smile (miles)
26. snap (naps)
27. stub (tubs)
28. owl (low)
29. heart (earth)
30. march (charm)

SECTION 3.

Pantomime Skits

In this section you will find not only skits but also suggestions for creating your own skits. The rules of pantomime apply to all the skits here, and no lines need be memorized, but some rehearsal will be necessary for top performance. The narrator (when a narrator is called for) can read his lines.

The following chart of stage positions will help you more clearly to direct the performance of others or to find your own stage positions. Use this guide whenever you need to establish or change a position on stage. All positions are given from the viewpoint of the actor as he faces the audience. It will help you to remember the difference between *up* stage and *down* stage by mentally picturing the stage as slanting downward toward the audience. *Down* stage is next to the audience.

(Audience here)

	Down stage left	Down stage center	Down stage right	
Left wing	Center stage left	Center stage	Center stage right	Right wing
	Up stage left	Up stage center	Up stage right	

(Back of stage here)

Add a few sound effects wherever possible. Have an off-stage sound man accompany the act with sounds such as bells, crashes, slammed doors, etc. The offstage sound should occur at exactly the same moment as the onstage action. A bit of practice will help your sound man to create effects that are just right.

In some cases it is a good idea to give your skit a musical background. The music should harmonize with the mood of the onstage action; for instance, merry music should accompany a merry scene. The music should not play so loudly that it takes away the attention of the audience from the performers. A record player or a pianist will serve nicely.

If you have no real stage or if your stage does not have a curtain, the players may show that their act has ended merely by bowing and exiting.

Exaggerate all movements, gestures, and facial expressions. Remember, your audience is at a distance. If you smile, make it a *wide* smile, if you are gay, show that you are *very* gay. Make every mood clearly mean what it is supposed to mean.

When one group of players is leading the action, the other players should more or less remain inactive. The audience can usually follow only one action at a time, so do not divide their attention.

Do not look directly at the viewers. When glancing in their direction, keep your eyes on a level slightly above their heads.

Watch your timing. Do not proceed with a second movement before the first movement is complete. Let each action tell its full story. Do not come onstage too early or too late. Do not permit an actor to interrupt the scene of another actor. Correct timing can be worked out during rehearsals.

When working out your skit, try to put yourself in the place of the audience. Ask yourself such questions as, "If I were out there, could I clearly see everything? . . . Would I know exactly what is supposed to be happening? . . . Could I

improve things by moving a bit faster or perhaps a bit slower?"
By answering your own questions you will surely build a popular skit.

Put everything you have into your performance, but remain relaxed about it. When the curtain goes down, try to find out just how and where you can sharpen your next performance. This is all it really takes to become a smooth and appreciated actor or actress.

SOLO SKITS

Here are a number of pantomime skits to be acted out by one person. The title of an act should be announced by the teacher or leader.

The Wrist Watch

1. Walk across stage, casually glance at your imaginary wrist watch, suddenly halt and stare at watch as if it has stopped.

2. Hold watch to ear, listen, shake head, wind watch, again listen and shake head.

3. Gently shake wrist, listen to watch, frown and shake head.

4. Gently tap watch with fingers, listen, shake head.

5. Sigh, shrug, take imaginary watch off wrist, again shrug as you hold it out, drop it on ground, jump on it several times.

6. Wave good-by to watch, walk away a few steps, suddenly halt, curiously cup hand to ear as if you think you hear the watch ticking.

7. Return to watch, pick it up, curiously hold it to ear, jerk back and stare at watch with pleased amazement, nod, quickly fasten watch on wrist, joyously hold up wrist, staring at watch as you walk off.

The Texas Cowboy

1. Enter as cowboy with coiled length of rope in hand.

2. Sight object about ten yards away, uncoil rope as you eagerly look at object.

3. Form a lasso, whirl rope overhead, toss rope, miss catching the object, let eyes follow fallen rope to ground, shake head in disappointment.

4. Pull rope back to you with both hands, again attempt to lasso object, again miss, again frown and tug rope back.

5. Carefully sight object, look very determined as you again whirl and toss.

6. Triumphantly cry out (in silent pantomime) as you catch object.

7. Tug object toward you with strained effort.

8. Clasp hands over head in satisfaction, forgetting that rope is still in your hand, feel sharp jerk, get pulled off stage with animal tugging you away.

The Golfer

1. Enter as golfer with imaginary golf club, search for ball, see it, walk to it.

2. Carefully study ball, walk over to hole which is about five yards away.

3. Take putting position, putt ball, watch it miss, shake head, frown.

4. Walk to ball, take aim, again miss, scowl.

5. Walk to ball, very carefully study, putt ball, hold hand to head in disappointment as you again miss.

6. Again walk to ball, carefully study, frown, look up and shake head, suddenly see something on other side of stage, throw club away, walk to other side of stage.

7. Pick up the gardener's shovel which you saw, smile, walk back to ball, dig a hole directly in front of ball, knock ball into hole with shovel, smile in satisfaction.

8. Take ball from hole, kiss it, notice shovel in hand, kiss it, sling shovel over shoulder, walk off with a gay step.

The Phonograph Record

1. Enter, take two or three records from shop display, examine them.

2. Search carefully for one record in particular.

3. Find your special record, set it on player, turn switch, set needle on record, listen with pleasure with hand cupped to ear.

4. Remove record, start to carry it to clerk, slip, fall, break record.

5. Look sadly down at broken pieces.

6. Take one piece at a time, carefully place them on phonograph, shove pieces with both palms as if pushing pieces into their original round shape.

7. Again place needle on pieces, listen with hand cupped to ear.

8. Nod in pleasant surprise as the record again plays.

9. One at a time, stuff pieces into pocket or bag.

10. Take money from wallet, pay clerk and happily exit.

Setting the Table

1. Enter carrying imaginary tablecloth, shake it out, spread it over table, smooth out wrinkles.

2. Pick up a pile of imaginary dishes, set them in various positions on the table.

3. Step back and study arrangements, shake head in displeasure, change positions of the dishes.

4. Repeat action of step 3 two more times.

5. Sigh in disappointment, gather up plates and pile them high in cradle of left arm.

6. Stiffly stand in back of table (facing audience), close eyes and carefully sail the dishes one at a time onto the table.

7. Open eyes, look at arrangement, grin with joy, nod, brush off hands, triumphantly exit.

The Colonel

1. As an army colonel reviewing marching troops, stand on a low platform (real, if possible) while at military attention.

2. Let head and eyes slowly move from your left to your right, then quickly turn to left again and once more slowly observe various imaginary groups as they march past.

3. Briskly salute two or three times.

4. Suddenly glare down at a particular soldier, step down to him, point finger at him, shake head in disapproval.

5. Indicate displeasure at the soldier's posture, march droopily in a small circle (with head bowed and arms flopping) to indicate that this is *not* the way to march.

6. Hold up finger before soldier to indicate that you will now show him the *right* way to march, then stiffly march in a small circle with chin held high and arms properly swinging, wag a finger at soldier and return to platform.

7. Watch parade for a moment, then quickly and briefly repeat action of steps 4, 5, and 6 with a second soldier, return to platform.

8. Move head and eyes from left to right with a broad movement and let head linger at right, looking into distance so as to indicate that the parade is over, stiffly turn body to right and salute departing soldiers, wave good-by.

9. Mop brow with handkerchief, return handkerchief to pocket, deeply sigh, step down and march off to left in the same droopy manner which you warned the soldiers against.

The Juggler

1. Hold up two fingers to indicate that you will first juggle just two balls.

2. Pick up imaginary balls, pretend to juggle them.

3. Hold up three fingers to indicate that you will next juggle three balls.

4. Pick up a third ball, juggle with a bit more difficulty.

5. Hold up five fingers to show that you will now juggle a total of five balls.

6. Juggle the five balls with a bit more difficulty than before.

7. Proudly hold up ten fingers.

8. Awkwardly gather several more balls into your hands and arms.

9. Drop a few of them, pick them up.

10. Take a deep sigh as if this is your one great effort.

11. Juggle with frantic and wild movements, such as leaping on to side to catch a falling ball and scooping a fallen ball from the floor.

12. Suddenly crouch, holding hands to top of head as if you are afraid the balls are crashing down upon you.

13. Look fearfully upward to see if there are any more coming down.

14. Rise, sadly hold up two fingers, pick up two balls and exit while juggling them.

The High Jumper

1. As a high jumper, crouch as you prepare to jump.

2. Run and try to leap over crossbar, knock it off, look down at it, snap fingers in disappointment, replace crossbar on its standards.

3. Repeat actions of step 2 two more times while showing your disappointment in varied ways, such as by groaning and sighing.

4. After third miss, suddenly get bright idea, walk a few steps away from high jump pit, pick up hammer and nails, return to pit, drive nails into crossbar so that it cannot fall off its standards.

5. Crouch, run, leap over crossbar, look back, shake hands above head in triumph, exit.

The Fisherman

1. Enter with imaginary fishing pole, sit on chair, prepare to fish.

2. Cast line into water, lean forward and peer at line as you eagerly await a bite.

3. Lean back as you get a mild tug on the line, reel in a fish with little effort, hold hands apart to indicate that the fish is at least a yard long, set fish down, again cast line.

4. Wait for a moment, get another mild tug, reel in the fish without any strain, again hold hands apart to indicate you have a fish about a yard long, set it down, again cast line.

5. Wait a moment, suddenly jerk backward as you get a violent tug on line, twist and squirm as you desperately reel in the powerful fish, take deep sigh as you land it.

6. Stare in amazement as you hold up fish, take it from line and hold hands apart to indicate that it is only two inches long.

7. Shake head in amazement as you stare at fish, give it an underhand toss and throw it back into water, point to water and flex muscles to indicate that it was certainly a powerful little fish, scoop up other fish, exit.

The Strong Man

1. As a strong man, enter with arms flexed and a powerful walk, face audience and bow.

2. Display arm muscles one at a time, bend down and grasp imaginary bar-bell with trembling arms, lift it overhead, lower it, bow.

3. Flex and display muscles of right arm, bend down and try to lift bar-bell with right arm, strain and drop it after lifting it only a few inches.

4. Look determined, briefly exercise right arm, bend down, again fail to lift bar-bell more than a few inches, scowl.

5. Shake head in disappointment, cup hand to mouth and pretend to call toward wing. (At this point an offstage assistant slides a small box onstage.)

6. Pick up box, hold it high so that audience can see its label which reads VITAMINS.

7. Scoop several handfuls of imaginary vitamins into mouth, swallow pills, set box down, flex muscles.

8. Stand over bar-bell, rub hands on trousers as if preparing for a great effort, bend down and succeed—after a mighty struggle—in lifting the bar-bell over head, lower it.

9. Take a step forward, bow to audience, try to casually scoop up vitamin box with one hand, amazingly find that it is too heavy, just barely lift box with both hands, struggle offstage with it.

Grandma Crosses the Street

1. As an elderly but spry lady, stand at the curb (a low box) with handbag tightly clutched.

2. Timidly turn head back and forth as you watch for an opportunity to cross the busy street.

3. Cautiously step off curb, start to cross, show alarm at approaching car, race back to curb, wag reproving finger after car.

4. Hold palm high for traffic to stop, try to cross, leap back to curb just in time.

5. Cautiously peer both ways, nod as you think you see an opening, quickly tiptoe into street a few steps, jerk about in confusion as cars whiz past, struggle back to curb, breathe heavily.

6. Sigh deeply in despair, hold finger to side of head and gaze slightly upward as if in deep thought, brighten and nod as you get a good idea.

7. Take a banana from handbag, slowly and clearly peel it, quickly eat the fruit, hold peel high to look at it, toss it so that it falls in the street about a foot from the curb.

8. Take a deep breath, deliberately step on peel, slip and slide forward as if the peel has enabled you to dodge the traffic, end up across the street.

9. Grin triumphantly, pick up peel, drop it in handbag, happily walk off.

TELEPHONE CHUCKLES

The group separates into couples. Each couple works out a pantomime skit centered about a telephone conversation. This skit may run from one to five minutes.

Players should try to build a simple story with a beginning, a middle, and an amusing conclusion. For instance, the plot might be that player A tries to get player B to speak louder on the phone. Player A indicates this by straining his ear at the receiver and by motioning upward. Player B then speaks louder and louder until—at the finish—he bellows so loud that he knocks his partner off his chair.

Partners may sit at tables or simply stand on opposite sides of the stage. The skit begins when one of the partners dials the phone and the other cups a hand to his ear and lifts the receiver.

Here are a few typical ideas:

1. Player A talks so long and so monotonously that player B drops his head and dozes.

2. Both talk excitedly and with sweeping gestures at the same time.

3. Player A wants to show player B something in a book, so player A holds an open book before the mouthpiece and points to the pages without speaking. Player B then nods as if seeing the pages.

4. Both open lunches and munch while conversing. They fumble awkwardly as they try to hold the phone while unwrapping a sandwich or opening a bottle. Player A speaks into a sandwich as if it were the mouthpiece; player B holds an apple to his ear as if it were the receiver.

5. Player A holds up a sheet of music and gaily sings, player B smacks his ear in pain and holds the receiver as far away from his ear as possible, then draws receiver close once

more, sways and smiles as he decides the singing is melodious after all.

6. Player A talks on and on without a single break, so player B yawns and rips pages off a calendar every few seconds.

7. Player A assumes a mischievous grin, tells player B to hold the line a moment, picks up a cat which he permits to meow into the phone. Player B reacts with bewilderment at the change in player A's "voice." (The cat can be real or imaginary. An imaginary cat can be indicated by gently picking it up from the floor with both hands and stroking it.)

8. Players chat for a while, rush off hurriedly and briefly to work—such as sweeping the floor—then rush back to phones. This can be repeated two or three times.

MIRROR STUNT

With a bit of practice this idea can be developed into a highly entertaining act. The idea is for two players to harmonize their pantomime movements so as to give the appearance of *one* player looking at his reflection in a full-length mirror. This means that both players comb their hair or brush their teeth in unison, just as if one player performed these movements in front of a mirror.

Here are notes and suggestions for building a superior performance.

1. Players face each other, sideways to the audience.

2. The two players should be approximately the same height and dress alike.

3. Practice a single movement until it is harmonious, then go on to the next one.

4. Practice all movements in slow motion at first, then speed up slightly. It is best if all movements are done with only moderate speed.

5. Choose broad, sweeping movements that can be clearly seen by the audience.

6. Keep feet planted in one place except when making definite foot movements.

7. Do not smile or laugh. (This makes it even funnier!)

8. Some typically amusing movements are: (a) Lean forward and touch noses as if peering closely into mirror. (b) Gaze in fond admiration by passing hand over hair and tilting head in a dramatic pose. (c) Players push palms together and rotate arms as if polishing the mirror. (d) Twist face into comical expressions. (e) Smile broadly.

9. The act may be given a funny finish by doing the following: Player A waves good-by but player B beckons "Come here." Player A then beckons "Come here" as player B waves good-by. They briefly stare in surprise at each other, shrug, face audience, bow in unison, exit.

BIRTHDAY SURPRISES

The aim of this pantomime skit is for a player to show all sorts of reactions and emotions at receiving a birthday present. He starts off by eagerly opening the package. The package is a real one which has been previously filled with the present by the performer. For convenience, the package should consist of a box which is already open at the top, although the performer pretends to unwrap and open it.

After opening the package he lifts the present from the box and goes into an act which includes a broad variety of exaggerated reactions such as joy, shock, bewilderment, amazement, gratitude, etc.

To build a comedy show, additional actors and actresses can come onstage one after another, look at the present and go through a series of emotions, too.

Here are twenty "presents" with suggestions for pantomime.

1. A shoe (wonder at the single shoe, take off own shoes, put on shoe, limp offstage)

2. A dog collar and leash (hold them out, pretend to call a dog from several directions, shrug as no dog appears, place collar around own neck and lead self off by leash)

3. A comic drawing (peer at it from several angles, laugh lightly, increase laughter until you are hysterically roaring, show picture to audience. NOTE: the picture can be of any comical nature, perhaps a scrawled drawing of the actor with his name beneath it)

4. A tattered, oversized jacket (hold it up in admiration, put it on, brush it off, proudly strut around)

5. A small rug (scratch head and wonder what to do with it, lay it on floor, walk down its length, turn around and pick it up, again lay it in front of you, again walk its length, continue to do this until you have walked offstage)

6. A pillow (lie down, set pillow under head, adjust its position several times, stretch, peacefully sleep)

7. A whiskbroom (go through fancy and funny motions while brushing yourself off—such as brushing your sleeve with dramatic sweeps and brushing off the soles of your shoes, also your elbows and ears)

8. A rope (test it by tugging on it, tie yourself up, happily skip around the stage for a moment or two, skip offstage)

9. A book (read while expressing a wide variety of emotions at the story, grow more excited as you turn pages, close book and sigh with emotional exhaustion)

10. A pencil or some other commonplace and inexpensive object (throw up arms in rapture as you peer into box, lift pencil, hold it up in deep admiration, hug it to chest while swaying in breathless joy)

11. A cube of wrapped butter (unwrap end of cube, take a slice of bread from pocket, rub butter over it, hungrily take a bite or two)

12. A jar labeled GLUE (dip fingers into imaginary glue, frown at your sticky fingers, rub them off on hip, find that your fingers are stuck to hip, try to pull them off with other hand)

13. An unshelled peanut (eagerly open a large box, throw inner wrappings aside, reach excitedly inside, pull out and hold up the peanut, look shocked, shrug, shell and eat peanut)

14. A balloon (playfully toss balloon into air, kick and swat it around, chase it offstage)

15. A small can labeled OIL (grin, pretend to oil your joints, such as elbows, knees, ankles, freely move joints to indicate that they now bend much easier)

16. A glass of water (gaze doubtfully at it as if wondering what to do with it, take a sip, wash your hands, pull a flower from your pocket and place it in glass, exit while sniffing flower)

17. A monster mask (put it on, stalk about stage while imitating a monster by clawing, creeping, grabbing, pretend to chase someone offstage)

18. A tube of toothpaste (nod in appreciation, take toothbrush from pocket, pretend to squeeze toothpaste onto toothbrush, vigorously pretend to brush teeth as you exit)

19. A dish of candy (eat a piece, react with pleasure at its delicious taste, eat another, suddenly become aware of viewers, pass dish down to them)

20. A large feather (playfully tickle your toes, chuckle, tickle your ear and laugh, quickly tickle yourself all over while silently roaring with merriment, exit while tickling and laughing)

WAITER!

Few situations offer such a fine opportunity for a pantomime comedy skit as that of a waiter serving a diner—or a group of diners. Any group can use the listed suggestions here, not necessarily in the same order. It would be even better for several groups to work out their acts and present them one after another. Make no mistake, they will all be different— and more hilarious than they look in print!

1. The diner cannot catch the waiter's attention.

2. The waiter spills imaginary foods and drinks on the diner.

3. The diner changes his order several times.

4. The waiter eats the diner's food.

5. The diner goes to sleep while waiting.

6. The waiter brings the wrong orders.

7. The diner helps himself to trays intended for another table.

8. The waiter hungrily watches the diner eat.

9. The diner chokes on the poor quality of food.

10. The waiter carries the food in his pocket.

11. The waiter sits with feet on table while taking the diner's order.

12. The diner complains of poor service.

13. The diner gets on hands and knees to plead for service.

14. The waiter drops dishes just as he is about to serve.

15. The waiter whisks up dishes just after the diner barely tastes them.

16. The diner chokes on hot food and hastily gulps water.

17. The waiter seasons the diner's food by pouring huge amounts of salt and pepper on it.

18. The waiter clears the table by tossing dishes over his shoulder.

19. The diner gets so hungry he takes off his necktie, sets it on plate, salts it, pretends to cut and eat it.

20. The waiter passes several times while holding fingers in ears so as not to hear diner's frantic calls.

21. The waiter pours water from pitcher into glass, drinks it himself.

22. The waiter, who has been sweeping the floor, brushes off diner with broom.

23. The diner finds he is without money to pay.

24. The waiter holds out hand for his tip and the diner pours water into waiter's palm.

25. The diner attempts to show the waiter how to serve and ends up sadly serving the waiter a full dinner.

SALESMAN!

Here is another situation which can easily be built into a funny skit. The idea is for the male customer to be trapped in a clothing store where he is the unwilling target of an eager salesman or group of salespeople. With some old clothes as "props" this skit becomes more realistic.

1. The customer innocently strolls along the sidewalk when the crouching salesman grabs him and pulls him into store.

2. The salesman locks the door after the customer.

3. The customer protests but the salesman distracts him by pointing out the fine clothes on display.

4. The salesman shakes his head in solemn disapproval of the customer's hat, coat, and tie, and removes them from customer.

5. The salesman forces all sorts of odd and ill-fitting clothes upon the customer.

6. The salesman is so pleased with one of the tattered coats which the customer rejects that he takes off his own coat and puts on the tattered one.

7. The customer tries to escape by crawling on hands and knees, but is caught and gently led back.

8. The customer weeps and pleads to be set free.

9. The salesman measures the customer in several peculiar ways, such as measuring the distance between his left ear and his right shoulder.

10. The customer selects a hat and sets it on his head, but the salesman shakes his head and turns the hat upside down on the customer's head.

11. The salesman removes customer's coat, slowly and deliberately tears it into shreds.

12. The salesman takes off customer's shoes, nods in appre-

ciation at them, removes his own shoes, replaces them with the customer's shoes.

13. The customer races for locked door, beats against it.

14. The salesman tries to cheer up the customer by peeling a banana and offering it to him.

15. The salesman takes a hat from box, throws away hat, places box on customer's head.

16. The customer gives up trying to resist, invites the salesman to sell him clothing.

17. The salesman finds that a coat is too narrow in the shoulders for the customer so he holds the customer's shoulders together, forces the coat on him.

18. The salesman displays exaggerated pride and admiration as he views the customer's appearance.

19. The salesman brings out several cans of paint, labeled with various colors, and brushes all over the customer's clothes. (Imaginary paint, of course.)

20. The salesman enthusiastically congratulates the customer by shaking his hand and slapping his back.

21. The salesman proudly escorts customer to mirror, customer looks at self in shock, salesman hastily leads him away from mirror.

22. The customer agrees with the salesman that he looks better (even though he doesn't).

23. The customer pays for clothing but the salesman holds out his hand for more and more.

24. The salesman grandly escorts the now-proud customer to the door, unlocks it.

25. The salesman and customer shake hands and the customer proudly exits wearing his tattered clothing.

DARING SAILORS

(A narrator reads the verses aloud while the players act according to the instructions. All the actions are performed quickly and briefly.)

One daring sailor sailed the ocean blue . . . (a player marches onstage, faces audience, steers ship) Along came a friend . . . (second player enters, they exchange greetings, stand alongside each other) And so there were two!

Two daring sailors sailed the stormy sea . . . (both steer at wheel while holding tight and swaying) They called and called for extra help . . . (as they call with cupped hands a third player joins them) And so there were three!

Three daring sailors stepped upon the shore . . . (players step forward, march in place) And when the three stepped back again . . . (as the three step back to original positions a fourth player joins them) The three had turned to four!

Four daring sailors did a fancy dive . . . (they make diving motions) They looked so fine and fancy . . . (fifth player enters, looks in admiration, joins them) That soon there were five!

Five daring sailors fished with crooked sticks . . . (they pretend to fish) Their dinner was so tasty . . . (as they pretend to eat a sixth player joins them) Very soon there were six!

Six daring sailors opened up a door . . . (they face wing and pretend to open doors) In jumped another friend . . . (seventh player jumps in) So there was one more!

Seven daring sailors all began to skate . . . (all pretend to skate) It looked so much like lots of fun . . . (eighth player skates onstage) That their number came to eight!

Eight daring sailors all stood in a line . . . (they line up at attention) And before they knew it . . . (ninth player quickly enters to join end of line) The line had stretched to nine!

Nine daring sailors wondered where they'd been . . . (they shade eyes with palms and gaze outward) Someone came to tell them . . . (tenth player enters, gestures outward) And that made ten!

Ten daring sailors all went swimming for fun . . . (all make swimming movements) And so they swam and swam and swam . . . (they swim offstage) Until at last there were none!

PAIRED SKITS

Pairs of players act out these pantomime skits, which may range in length from a few seconds to three or four minutes. Performers should take as much time as possible to work out a skit in which the actions are both clear and funny. Each act is announced. The first one, for example, would be introduced: "In this skit, we see a frantic barber as he tries to cut the hair of a wriggling boy."

1. Barber cuts hair of wriggling boy
2. Doctor and patient
3. Mailman and lady-of-the-house
4. Grocery clerk and customer
5. Cowboy tries to rope wild horse
6. Carpenter and his assistant
7. Taxi driver and passenger
8. Dancer and awkward partner
9. Swimming instructor and student
10. Pedestrian asks directions of policeman
11. Sprinter and track coach
12. Lion tamer and ferocious lion
13. Mother teaches her daughter to cook
14. Pianist and singer
15. Bank teller and customer
16. Lady tries to escape angry bee
17. Tight-rope walker and spectator
18. Baseball pitcher and catcher
19. Boss dictates letter to secretary
20. Father tries to soothe crying baby
21. Driving teacher and student driver
22. Fisherman tries to catch cautious fish
23. Play director shows student how to act
24. Man tries to teach dog to shake hands

SKITS OF FAMOUS EVENTS

Players pantomime famous events of history. In most cases it would be best to announce the event beforehand; however, in a few instances the viewers may be allowed to guess what event is taking place.

Offstage music may be played in keeping with the mood of the action; for example, a patriotic theme may accompany Washington and his soldiers as they march offstage.

A complete show may be presented by assigning skits to several groups or classes. Costumes will help in setting the right atmosphere.

Basic movements for each event are supplied. The leader may wish to add extra touches wherever they will add to the effectiveness of the skit.

Washington at Valley Forge

1. Cold and tattered soldiers are sitting and lying on the ground.

2. Women enter to feed, clothe, and bandage them.

3. Washington enters, looks about in concern.

4. A few of the healthier soldiers struggle to their feet to salute him.

5. Washington passes from soldier to soldier, patting each and speaking words of comfort.

6. A dispatch rider races in, hands a message to Washington.

7. Washington peers offstage as if observing enemy troop movements.

8. Washington becomes alert, signals to a bugler who steps forward.

9. As the bugle sounds the soldiers struggle to their feet, grab their rifles.

10. Soldiers form a marching column.

11. The flag is advanced to the front of the column.

12. Washington gestures outward to indicate that they will march forward to victory.

13. Washington places himself at head of troops.

14. With heads held high, the soldiers follow Washington offstage.

California Gold Discovery

1. Three or four miners dig for gold.

2. One finds a large nugget, holds it high, shouts.

3. Others excitedly crowd about him while shouting and gesturing.

4. Several more miners rush onstage to see nugget.

5. All dig furiously on various parts of stage.

6. More miners rush in to join them.

7. Two or three miners also find large nuggets, hold them up.

8. Some miners race off with nuggets, others continue to dig.

First Flight of the Wright Brothers

1. The Wright Brothers work on their airplane.
2. They make arm movements to each other which indicate flight.
3. They again work on airplane, discuss various parts.
4. Curious neighbors enter to watch.
5. The onlookers talk among themselves, make motions which indicate flight.
6. The Wright Brothers shake hands, look skyward.
7. One of brothers pantomimes the act of piloting; he flies offstage.
8. Other brother races off after the airplane, exits.
9. Neighbors look upward and offstage in amazement as they watch the flight.
10. Brothers return onstage.
11. Neighbors crowd around to congratulate Wright Brothers.

Building of the Panama Canal

1. Surveyors enter, survey the land.

2. Workers enter to dig, shovel, haul earth.

3. Foreman enters, makes gestures to indicate the course of the canal.

4. Foreman instructs and encourages various workers.

5. Workers labor on either side of partially completed canal.

6. Two or three distinguished-looking men (government officials) enter and look about in approval.

7. Workers halt; players stand on either side of finished canal.

8. All turn toward wing and eagerly watch.

9. A large paper boat (carried by players who walk in back of it) sails across stage as if through canal.

10. All players cheer and congratulate each other as ship sails across stage.

11. All players happily follow ship offstage.

Lincoln's Gettysburg Address

1. A crowd enters and gathers about a platform.
2. A few soldiers march in, form a guard about the platform.
3. Several government officials enter, take chairs on platform.
4. Lincoln solemnly enters, is saluted by an army officer.
5. Lincoln is greeted by government officials.
6. He sits in center of platform.
7. A speaker pantomimes an introduction of Lincoln.
8. Lincoln stands before audience as if preparing to speak.
9. As Lincoln silently gazes over audience—without pantomime of any kind—an offstage voice recites his Gettysburg Address.
10. Lincoln steps back, is again greeted by officials.
11. Lincoln is escorted offstage by soldiers and officials.

Columbus' Discovery of America

1. A crewman stands at ship's wheel and turns it.
2. Columbus enters, stands with arms behind back while gazing seaward.
3. His crew approaches as he continues to gaze.
4. The crew surrounds him, angrily arguing.
5. Columbus solemnly shakes his head, gestures seaward.
6. The crew grumbles, draws back from Columbus.
7. A crew member separates himself from the others, walks to rail, peers through telescope.
8. He shouts, points outward, calls the attention of the others.
9. All except Columbus race to rail, peer outward, cheer.
10. A crew member joyously escorts Columbus to rail.
11. Columbus peers at land through telescope, gratefully nods.
12. Part of crew congratulates Columbus.
13. Another part of crew happily gazes toward land.
14. Third part of crew hoists more sail and excitedly works about ship.

The Pilgrims' First Thanksgiving

1. Pilgrims enter with food, set outdoor table.
2. A Pilgrim rushes in, indicates that friendly Indians are approaching.
3. Pilgrims welcome several Indians.
4. Pilgrims and Indians chat as dinner is further prepared.
5. Pilgrims escort Indians to table; all sit.
6. All bow heads as standing Pilgrim leads in brief prayer.
7. Dinner and conversation is enjoyed by all.
8. All rise.
9. Pilgrims and Indians exchange greetings of friendship.
10. Pilgrims wave good-by as Indians leave.
11. Pilgrims happily clear table and exit.

The Boston Tea Party

1. Players enter from several directions, gather in stage center.
2. They huddle, glance furtively about, quietly talk.
3. They disguise themselves as Indians.
4. They row to a ship on opposite side of stage.
5. They climb ship's deck.
6. They rush about, toss boxes into sea.
7. They row back to shore.
8. They remove disguises, go separate ways.

The Ride of Paul Revere

1. Several citizens pretend to sleep.
2. Paul Revere rides in with shouts and gestures.
3. The citizens rise, look about in surprise and alarm.
4. Paul Revere knocks on door after door.
5. Citizens open windows, peer out.
6. Paul Revere makes motions which indicate that the British are coming.
7. Citizens quickly dress, dash into street.
8. Paul Revere rides offstage.

THE MAN WHO DIDN'T LIKE RAIN

CHARACTERS: Narrator
The Man Who Didn't Like Rain
Farmer
Fish
Schoolchildren (two or more)
Weatherman
Robin

SETTING: Outdoors. A chair is set upstage center.

NARRATOR (enters, stands near wing): Ladies and gentlemen . . . there was once a man who didn't like rain. He liked trees and rivers and flowers and lakes, but he just *didn't* like rain. He didn't like showers nor drizzles nor downpours . . . (sadly shake head). He didn't even like pitters and patters. As you can see . . . (gesture to wing as Man enters) he just didn't like rain of any kind. (Man enters with a large sign reading DOWN WITH RAIN! He scowls at sky, glumly takes position alongside Narrator.)

NARRATOR: He didn't like rain because it got him wet all over . . . (Man angrily brushes raindrops from face and shoulders) and because it made him slip when he walked . . . (Man slips about a few steps) and because he couldn't go out to water his garden. (Man sways imaginary garden hose while scowling skyward.)

NARRATOR: So the man who didn't like rain spent most of his time just sitting around. (Man sits on chair with sign propped on knees. He gestures skyward for the rain to go away.)

NARRATOR: One day as he sat in the rain, he saw a happy farmer gathering some fruits and vegetables. (Farmer enters with basket, sets it down, smiles at raining sky, digs potatoes and picks fruit, exits with heavy basket.)

NARRATOR: He also saw a gay little fish swimming in the

big, big river. The river was getting even bigger and bigger because of the heavy rain. (Fish enters with swimming motions, swims gaily about, swims offstage.)

NARRATOR: And then he saw some youngsters having lots of fun playing in the rain. (Children briskly enter to perform various fun-in-the-rain stunts, such as cupping hands to catch rain, hopping over puddles, splashing water on each other.) One little boy thought it was a good time to get clean! (A boy stands stage center, pulls towel and soap from pocket, scrubs himself—without disrobing! Children exit.)

NARRATOR: Then he saw that hard-working fellow, the weatherman! (Weatherman solemnly enters with upraised umbrella, halts at stage center, faces audience. Three times he holds out a palm, wipes wet hand on his coat, nods, unfolds and reveals to audience a large sheet of paper which reads, RAIN PREDICTED. He solemnly exits.)

NARRATOR: And finally the man who didn't like rain saw a thirsty little robin who needed a drink of rain-water. (Robin flies in, hops about, goes through the motions of drinking from a pool, hops offstage.)

NARRATOR: All these things caused the man who didn't like rain to *think* . . . (Man thinks by peering curiously at sky) and *think* . . . (Man stands, thinks harder) and *think!* (Man thinks very hard by pacing the floor with head bowed and hands clasped at back.) He began to think that rain might be pretty good after all. He thought of all the good things it gave to the world. Like vegetables . . . (Farmer enters, freezes in digging position) and rivers . . . (Fish enters, holds swimming pose) and playtime . . . (Children rush in, freeze in play positions) and weather reports . . . (Weatherman enters, holds outstretched palm) and water to drink . . . (Robin flits in, holds drinking pose.)

NARRATOR: All of a sudden, the man who didn't like rain started really to *like* rain. He smiled at the sky . . . (Man smiles upward) and smiled even more. (Man broadens smile) He even laughed! (Man laughs, joyously throws arms skyward.)

NARRATOR (excitedly): So he went out and had fun in the rain just like everyone else!

(Man races in turn to each of the others, briefly acts out their frozen positions, races to his sign DOWN WITH RAIN, holds it up to audience with one hand while wildly gesturing skyward for the rain to come down. As he finishes, the others exit while acting out their roles—for example, the Farmer walks off while picking fruit. The Man gaily skips offstage while happily holding high his sign.)

NARRATOR: And that is how the man who once said (frown) down with rain, finally said (smile) *down with rain!* (bow and exit.)

THE TAKE-TURNERS

CHARACTERS: Narrator
Mr. Melody, a pianist

Do
Re
Mi
Fa
Sol
La
Ti
Do
} Musical Notes

SETTING: The Musical Notes are lined up facing audience. A chair is set in front of them. A few items which indicate a musical theme, such as instruments or sheet music, may be set in the background.

NARRATOR: Ladies and gentlemen, we would like you to see —and hear—an exciting story. The story is about eight young musical notes who lived inside a piano. (Gesture to Notes who briefly and awkwardly jump up and down in unison.) Their names are Do, Re, Mi, Fa, Sol, La, Ti, and Do. As you can see, the Notes are all played at the same time—they had not as yet learned how to take turns playing. (Notes again jump in unison.) Our story is also about Mr. Melody, a world-famous pianist. (Gesture to Mr. Melody who enters, bows to audience, sits in chair facing Notes.)

NARRATOR: One day Mr. Melody sat down to play a lovely piece of music. (Mr. Melody pretends to play by striking an imaginary keyboard. As the Musical Notes awkwardly jump up and down, more or less in unison, an actual offstage pianist plays a few notes in disharmony.)

NARRATOR (dismayed): What is this? What has happened? This isn't a lovely song. (to Mr. Melody) Mr. Melody, please try again. (Mr. Melody again plays with the same discordant result.)

NARRATOR (to audience): Perhaps Mr. Melody has not shown the musical notes how to take turns. (to Mr. Melody) Mr. Melody, did you notice that all the notes played at the same time? Perhaps you should show them how to take turns. Once they know how to be *take-turners* I am sure we will have a lovely song. (Mr. Melody nods. As he taps each note, one at a time and going upscale, the notes jump up in turn. The offstage pianist taps notes accordingly. The action is then repeated downscale.)

NARRATOR (pleased): Now that they are *take-turners* I am sure we will have a lovely song. Try again, Mr. Melody. (Mr. Melody plays a slow piece as the notes jump up and down. Note: they jump in any order and not in unison, much as actual notes might move. The result is a melody.)

NARRATOR (brightly): And that is just about the end of our story. The *take-turners* have learned how to make a merry melody by taking turns. So they play (music plays as Notes happily jump in rapid movements) and play . . . and play. (as music ends, all bow and exit.)

THE HAPPY HIKERS

CHARACTERS: Narrator

Happy Hikers (as many as desired)

SETTING: Bare stage. The Happy Hikers stand in various stage positions, facing audience.

NARRATOR (gesturing to Hikers): Ladies and gentlemen, meet our happy hikers! (Hikers smile, wave to audience, hike in place. Note: all movements are in place.) Let's watch their adventures as they hike through the woods and over the mountains. There they go! (Hikers increase pace slightly.)

NARRATOR (as he looks at Hikers): Looks like they're climbing a steep hill! (Hikers bend backward as if climbing.) They're on top! What a lovely view! (Hikers look around in appreciation.) Now watch them get down! (Hikers slip and slide as if plunging downhill.) They must be out of breath! (Hikers hold hands on chests, breathe heavily.)

NARRATOR: Now they're passing through a meadow. (Hikers walk, then halt. Narrator peers closely at Hikers.) What do they see? A rabbit! (Hikers swiftly glance from left to right.) And a meadow lark! (Hikers quickly glance from ground to sky.) And a bumblebee! (Hikers jerk heads and eyes about. Narrator cries out a warning.) Watch out for the bumblebee! (Hikers run swiftly in place, waving arms as if battling off bumblebee.)

NARRATOR: As I said, they are *happy* hikers, happy because of the beautiful mountains they see . . . (Hikers happily shield eyes with palms and peer.) And because of all that clean, fresh air they breathe . . . (Hikers happily breathe while expanding their chests.) And especially because they got away from that buzzing bumblebee! (Hikers smile and nod, turn heads slightly to rear, wave good-by to the bumblebee.)

NARRATOR: Looks like they are tired from all that hiking. (Hikers slow down, walk droopily. Narrator excitedly waves outward as he peers ahead.) There's just what they need—a cool, refreshing drink from the river. (to Hikers) Can you make it to the river, Happy Hikers? (Hikers nod, pick up speed, kneel down at river, drink, scoop water over their faces.)

NARRATOR: Ah! How refreshing! On your way, Happy Hikers! (Hikers rise. Narrator speaks to them with caution.) Try to jump all the way across that river—keep those little tootsies dry! (Hikers jump but look down in dismay as they shake their wet feet. Narrator speaks sympathetically.) Don't feel too bad about not making it—after all, that river was more than a block wide. At least you have cool toes.

NARRATOR (as he looks ahead): Look what's in front of them—a fork in the road. Hope they take the right road. (Hikers turn somewhat to left.) No, they took the *left* road.

Well, maybe the *left* road is the *right* road . . . (Narrator is confused by his own speech.) I mean . . . maybe the *right* one is the *wrong* one and the *left* one is the *right* one . . . (Narrator shakes head.) Maybe we'd better just see what happens . . . (Hikers turn in circles as they march in place; some turn in left circles, some in right circles. The Narrator is distressed.) They're lost! I guess the *right* road was the *left* road after all . . . hmmm, I'd better not start that again. (Narrator sighs in relief as Hikers again march straight ahead.) Looks like all is right . . . I mean, all is *well*.

NARRATOR: I wonder when they will stop for lunch? (Hikers suddenly stop, keep heads and eyes straight ahead, reach into pockets, bring imaginary bits of food to lips, munch briefly, take handkerchiefs from pockets, quickly pat lips, replace handkerchiefs, resume marching. Note: this action should be done in unison or with as much unison as possible. The Narrator shakes his head in surprise.) Guess they weren't very hungry.

NARRATOR: Look! A lovely lake. (to audience) I wonder if they will hike around it or swim across? Let's see . . . (Hikers sit on floor as if getting into rowboats, make rowing motions. The Narrator smiles, shrugs.) I guess that's better than trying to *hike* across. (Hikers stand, resume marching.)

NARRATOR (peers at trail): Look at that crooked trail ahead! Nothing but twists and turns! (Hikers twist and turn in various directions as they march. Note: this need not be done in unison; players twist about individually. After a few seconds they resume their forward march. Narrator sighs.) I'm glad that's over—I was getting dizzy.

NARRATOR: Looks like they have come to the end of the trail. I wonder what their final destination is? (Narrator speaks to Hikers.) Say, Happy Hikers, wait a minute. (Hikers halt.) Now that you have reached the end of your hike, what are you going to do next? (Hikers grin broadly, march with a higher and livelier step than before. The Narrator staggers as if fainting, painfully holds his head.) You mean that the next thing you are going to do is to *march some more?* (Hikers vigorously nod their heads. The Narrator apologetically speaks to audience.) I'm sorry folks, but I just can't keep up with them any longer. Good-by. (Narrator waves to Hikers.) And a happy hike to you, Happy Hikers. (Narrator weakly exits at right. The Hikers face left, march off while keeping heads and eyes turned offstage, wave farewell to audience.)

HOW MUSIC MADE EVERYONE HAPPY

CHARACTERS: The Very Lonely Man

The Very Nice Children (as many as desired)

SETTING: A single chair is set at left stage, a number of others chairs are set in semicircle at right stage. Note: Actual music may be added to the skit if desired. If an offstage piano or other instrument is employed, it may be played in unison with the children's pantomimes.

NARRATOR (enters, stands near left wing): There was once a very lonely man. (Man feebly enters from left, sits.) Next door was a school. (Children enter from right, sit.) The very lonely man was very sad because he had no one to play music for him. He wished and wished for someone to play. (Man sadly nods.) And the very nice children were very sad because they had no one for whom they could play their music. They wished and wished for someone to hear their music. (Children sadly nod in unison.)

NARRATOR: One day the very lonely man said to himself, *I will open my window. Maybe someone will send music into my home.* So he opened his window. (Man opens window at stage center, returns to chair.) And on that very same day the very nice children said, *We will open a school window. Maybe someone will listen to our music.* So one of the boys opened a school window. (Boy opens window at stage center.)

NARRATOR: So the very lonely man listened. (Man cups hand at ear toward window.) And the very nice children played . . . first the trombone . . . (trombonist pantomimes) then the violinist . . . (violinist pantomimes) then the kettle drums . . . (drummer pantomimes.) Then *all* the musicians played! (All pantomime various instruments.)

NARRATOR: So the very lonely man was not sad or lonely any more. (Man briskly beats time and sways to the music.) And the very nice children were not sad any more. (Children smile, play spiritedly.) The happy man kept his window open from that day on. And so did the very nice children. (All bow and exit).

THE CHILDREN WHO FOUND
NEW FRIENDS

CHARACTERS: Narrator
Western Children (as many as desired)
Indian Children (about equal in number to
Western Children)

SETTING: Outdoors during days of early West. A few bushes, buckets and similar items will help to indicate the period. A river, which splits the stage from upstage to downstage, is indicated by lengths of rippled rope set a few feet apart.

NARRATOR: Many years ago some pioneer children journeyed to the West with their parents. One morning they ran from their covered wagons to play in the wide, lazy river. (Western Children rush in from the right, play between the right wing and their side of the river bank. They recognize the river by wading near the shore, drinking, splashing water on each other.)

NARRATOR: On that very same morning a band of Indian Children came down from the hills to play in the wide, lazy river. (Indian Children enter from left, also play about.)

NARRATOR: The Western Children heard some strange noises coming from the other side of the river, so they stopped to listen. (Western Children halt, listen with hands cupped to ears.)

NARRATOR: And so did the Indian Children. (Indian Children also halt, listen.)

NARRATOR: One little Western boy waded to the middle of the river to take a look. (Western boy wades to center of river, peers by raising palm to brow, throws up arms in fright, rushes back in alarm, tells others of Indians. The Western Children excitedly peer and chatter with each other while gesturing across the river.)

NARRATOR: And a little Indian boy decided to see who was making all the noise on the other side of his river. (Indian boy duplicates action of Western boy. The Indian Children also talk it over excitedly.)

NARRATOR: The Western Children were so frightened by the Indian Children that they ran off! (Western Children rush offstage.) And the Indian Children were so frightened of the Western Children that they also scooted away! (Indian Children run offstage.)

NARRATOR: Now this was a very sad thing. None of the children could enjoy the wide, lazy river any more. It's too bad they were so scared of each other! (sadly close book, shake head.) So I guess that is the end of the story . . . (happily uplift head as a Western girl timidly enters, speak hopefully.) Wait a minute . . . looks like there's more to the story . . . let's see what happens . . . (The Western girl cautiously peers across the river, slowly wades to its center, waves at the hiding Indian Children. An Indian girl timidly enters, pauses, waves back, wades to center of river where the girls stand opposite each other. They shyly look each other over, touch each other's hair, finally smile and pat each other in a gesture of friendship. Both turn, gesture for the others to come. Two more children from each camp enter and repeat the gestures of friendship and welcome. All six now turn and enthusiastically wave to the rest who rush out to meet and mingle. Western Children pair off with Indian Children and they play together.)

NARRATOR: And that is *really* the end of the story . . . a very happy ending, don't you think? (All bow and exit.)

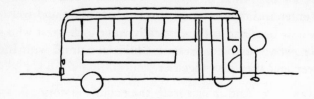

THE BUS

The purpose of this is to build a pantomime play around a bus, its driver and passengers. This is a familiar situation which the players can develop into an entertaining pantomime running for 15 to 20 minutes. It is excellent for large groups, inasmuch as an endless number of passengers can enter and exit.

The play director first gets the actors and actresses together to work out a series of incidents and happenings aboard the bus. The incidents are then acted out one after another to form the total pantomime play. Listed below are fifteen basic situations which can be easily developed into funny and surprising scenes. Players can think of others.

The stage is set with rows of chairs representing bus seats, with a different type of chair at the front representing the driver's seat. Have two rows of chairs with an aisle between them. The play director should make sure that the chairs are so arranged that the audience can see the actions clearly. A good arrangement is to slant the chairs from upstage left to down-stage right.

1. A lady passenger fumbles so awkwardly in her handbag for her fare that she spills packages all over the defense-less driver.

2. Three passengers scramble for a single seat. They end up trying to share it.

3. At one stop, all of the passengers get off at the rear door and immediately re-enter from the front. They do this casually, as if it were the normal thing to do.

4. The weary driver tries to explain directions to a lady passenger who just does not seem to understand.

5. Passengers bounce up and down as the bus hits a bumpy road. Some of them bounce across the aisle to exchange seats.

6. A beggar enters, pantomimes the fact that he has no money. He entertains the passengers with a brief dance, passes his hat for a collection, pays his fare and sits down.

7. A passenger insists on telling the driver how to drive. The driver finally gives up by placing the shocked passenger in the driver's seat while he, the driver, relaxes among the passengers.

8. A passenger enters with arms outstretched as if walking in his sleep. He pays his fare, walks to a seat and sleeps. After several other scenes have been performed by other players he rises and exits, still walking in his sleep.

9. The driver pulls to a halt, opens his lunch box, casually eats. An impatient passenger angrily protests while pointing to his watch. The driver offers him a slice of cake which is so delicious the passenger forgets all about the time.

10. An actor in the costume and mask of a monkey boards the bus to cause all sorts of confusion. He tries to sit in the lap of a frightened lady or chases someone out of the rear door of the bus.

11. A pair of players dressed as swordsmen enter while dueling (with imaginary swords). They halt long enough to pay their fares casually, then resume dueling down the aisle and out of the rear door.

12. A small child insists on offering his lollipop to the driver. When the driver frantically refuses, the child continues to insist by rubbing the imaginary lollipop into the driver's face and hair.

13. The bus driver makes wide turns and sudden halts. The passengers sway or fall forward or perform other movements according to the driver's actions.

14. The first man in line at a bus stop is crowded onto the bus by those behind him. He is further crowded down the aisle and out of the rear door.

15. A lady standing in the aisle uses every trick possible to get the attention of a seated man (in hopes he will prove gallant), but he carefully avoids taking the hint.

Index